BAR 19-87

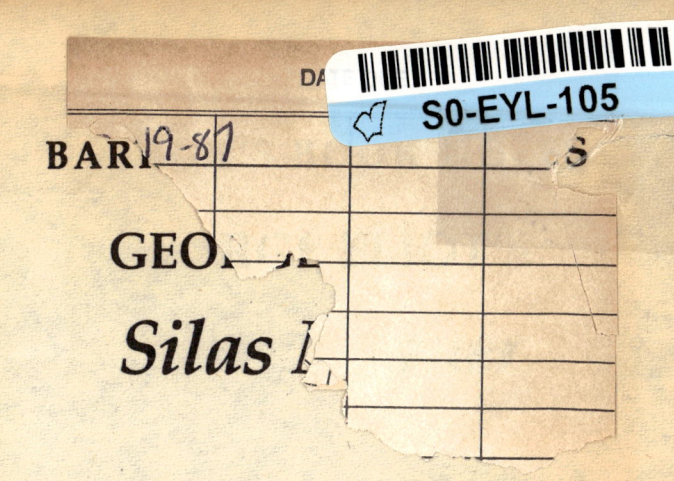

GEO

Silas

DISCARD

HORSESHOE BEND REGIONAL LIBRARY
203 WEST STREET
DADEVILLE, ALABAMA 36853

BARRON'S BOOK NOTES

GEORGE ELIOT'S
Silas Marner

BY

Holly Hughes

SERIES COORDINATOR

Murray Bromberg
Principal, Wang High School of Queens
Holliswood, New York

Past President
High School Principals Association of New York City

124827 ✓

BARRON'S EDUCATIONAL SERIES, INC.
Woodbury, New York • London • Toronto • Sydney

ACKNOWLEDGMENTS

Our thanks to Milton Katz and Julius Liebb for their advisory assistance on the *Book Notes* series.

© Copyright 1985 by Barron's Educational Series, Inc.

All rights reserved.
No part of this book may be reproduced in any form, by photostat, microfilm, xerography, or any other means, or incorporated into any information retrieval system, electronic or mechanical, without the written permission of the copyright owner.

All inquiries should be addressed to:
Barron's Educational Series, Inc.
113 Crossways Park Drive
Woodbury, New York 11797

Library of Congress Catalog Card No. 85-4069

International Standard Book No. 0-8120-3538-0

Library of Congress Cataloging in Publication Data

Hughes, Holly.
  George Eliot's Silas Marner.

  (Barron's book notes)
  Bibliography: p. 107
  Summary: A guide to reading "Silas Marner" with a critical and appreciative mind encouraging analysis of plot, style, form, and structure. Also includes background on the author's life and times, sample tests, term paper suggestions, and a reading list.
  1. Eliot, George, 1819-1880. Silas Marner.
  [1. Eliot, George, 1819-1880. Silas Marner.
  2. English literature—History and criticism] I. Title.
  II. Series.
  PR4670.H8   1985   823'.8   85-4069
  ISBN 0-8120-3538-0

PRINTED IN THE UNITED STATES OF AMERICA

567 550 987654321

CONTENTS

Advisory Board	vii
How to Use This Book	ix
THE AUTHOR AND HER TIMES	1
THE NOVEL	7
The Plot	7
The Characters	9
Other Elements	20
Setting	20
Themes	22
Style	25
Point of View	27
Form and Structure	28
The Story	29
A STEP BEYOND	95
Tests and Answers	95
Term Paper Ideas and other Topics for Writing	105
Further Reading	107
Critical Works	107
Author's Other Works	109
Glossary	109
The Critics	111

ADVISORY BOARD

We wish to thank the following educators who helped us focus our *Book Notes* series to meet student needs and critiqued our manuscripts to provide quality materials.

Sandra Dunn, English Teacher
Hempstead High School, Hempstead, New York

Lawrence J. Epstein, Associate Professor of English
Suffolk County Community College, Selden, New York

Leonard Gardner, Lecturer, English Department
State University of New York at Stony Brook

Beverly A. Haley, Member, Advisory Committee
National Council of Teachers of English Student
Guide Series, Fort Morgan, Colorado

Elaine C. Johnson, English Teacher
Tamalpais Union High School District
Mill Valley, California

Marvin J. LaHood, Professor of English
State University of New York College at Buffalo

Robert Lecker, Associate Professor of English
McGill University, Montréal, Québec, Canada

David E. Manly, Professor of Educational Studies
State University of New York College at Geneseo

Bruce Miller, Associate Professor of Education
State University of New York at Buffalo

Frank O'Hare, Professor of English and
Director of Writing
Ohio State University, Columbus, Ohio

Faith Z. Schullstrom, Member, Executive Committee
National Council of Teachers of English
Director of Curriculum and Instruction
Guilderland Central School District, New York

Mattie C. Williams, Director, Bureau of Language Arts
Chicago Public Schools, Chicago, Illinois

HOW TO USE THIS BOOK

You have to know how to approach literature in order to get the most out of it. This *Barron's Book Notes* volume follows a plan based on methods used by some of the best students to read a work of literature.

Begin with the guide's section on the author's life and times. As you read, try to form a clear picture of the author's personality, circumstances, and motives for writing the work. This background usually will make it easier for you to hear the author's tone of voice, and follow where the author is heading.

Then go over the rest of the introductory material—such sections as those on the plot, characters, setting, themes, and style of the work. Underline, or write down in your notebook, particular things to watch for, such as contrasts between characters and repeated literary devices. At this point, you may want to develop a system of symbols to use in marking your text as you read. (Of course, you should only mark up a book you own, not one that belongs to another person or a school.) Perhaps you will want to use a different letter for each character's name, a different number for each major theme of the book, a different color for each important symbol or literary device. Be prepared to mark up the pages of your book as you read. Put your marks in the margins so you can find them again easily.

Now comes the moment you've been waiting for—the time to start reading the work of literature. You may want to put aside your *Barron's Book Notes* volume until you've read the work all the way through. Or you may want to alternate, reading the *Book Notes* analysis of each section as soon as you have finished reading the corresponding part of the original. Before you move on, reread crucial passages you don't fully understand. (Don't take this guide's analysis for granted—make up your own mind as to what the work means.)

Once you've finished the whole work of literature, you may want to review it right away, so you can firm up your ideas about what it means. You may want to leaf through the book concentrating on passages you marked in reference to one character or one theme. This is also a good time to reread the *Book Notes* introductory material, which pulls together insights on specific topics.

When it comes time to prepare for a test or to write a paper, you'll already have formed ideas about the work. You'll be able to go back through it, refreshing your memory as to the author's exact words and perspective, so that you can support your opinions with evidence drawn straight from the work. Patterns will emerge, and ideas will fall into place; your essay question or term paper will almost write itself. Give yourself a dry run with one of the sample tests in the guide. These tests present both multiple-choice and essay questions. An accompanying section gives answers to the multiple-choice questions as well as suggestions for writing the essays. If you have to select a term paper topic, you may choose one from the list of suggestions in this book. This guide also provides you with a reading list, to help you when you start research for a term paper, and a selection of provocative comments by critics, to spark your thinking before you write.

THE AUTHOR AND HER TIMES

George Eliot was not her real name. She was born in 1819 as Marian (or Mary Anne) Evans, the youngest child of a prosperous estate manager in the rural English Midlands. Even as a child, it was apparent that she was very bright—and unfortunately homely. She craved affection, but her proud, strong-willed mother showed her little love. Her father was fond of her but was often too busy to pay her any attention. And so she clung dearly to her older brother Isaac, her constant childhood companion. Playing in the meadows and by the riverbanks of an unspoiled, fertile countryside, she found happiness of a kind.

When they grew up, however, Isaac became narrow-minded and conservative, and he felt little in common with his bookish sister. Marian had become simply a provincial, middle-class old maid. In a society where wifehood and motherhood were still the main roles for women, an unmarried daughter in her twenties like Marian was in many ways a second-class citizen. Her older brothers and sisters all moved away and started their own families. After Mrs. Evans died, Marian was left alone with her father. In ailing health, he retired, left the country home Marian loved, and moved to the nearby city of Coventry. There, Marian's days were spent in charitable "good works" and in keeping house. Between jam-making and needlework, visiting the poor, and nursing her crotchety father, she had little time to herself. Yet she managed somehow to read books—poetry (especially Wordsworth and Shakespeare), novels, and dense works of theology and philosophy, in several languages.

Soon, however, Marian made friends with Coventry's most progressive thinkers, who encouraged her intellectual interests. One day she calmly announced to her father that she would no longer go to church with him, since she didn't believe in God anymore. Apparently this change had been brewing in her mind for some time, but it was a surprise and an outrage to conventional Mr. Evans. Only after several weeks of family tension did Marian give in, reasoning with herself that, if she didn't believe in Christianity, it was no sin to go to church just to keep the peace.

Rejecting Christianity was still a daring thing for a single woman to do in nineteenth-century England. It would ruin her marriage prospects, as well as her chances of obtaining a teaching job (teaching was one of the few careers open to women). Luckily, however, Marian's new friends introduced her to a circle of people who shared some of her unorthodox views.

While most of the English still followed Queen Victoria in preserving the values of home, church, and empire, new ideas were beginning to sweep through England. Scientific discoveries were shattering established ideas about the natural world. (Charles Darwin's revolutionary *On the Origin Of Species by Means of Natural Selection* would be published in 1859.) Not only nature, but human social systems as well, were subjected to scientific analysis. Theories such as social Darwinism, rational humanism, and Marxism would eventually grow out of this. Philosophers were suggesting entirely new moral systems to go with the revolutionary scientific views. In place of an orderly universe ruled by God, justice, and the class system, these Victorians contemplated the possibility of a vast, bleak void where nothing but scientific principles applied.

This was a heady environment for Marian Evans. Her new friends, impressed by her powerful mind, gave her a sense of self-worth. Eventually she was asked to translate a book, then to write reviews for intellectual journals. After her father died she moved to London and began to edit one such journal. In the thick of the literary scene, admired by famous people, she came into her own. Interesting men paid her attention; she had a couple of awkward romances. Then she fell in love with George Henry Lewes, a prominent journalist and critic—and a married man.

Lewes fell in love with her, too, but under the laws of those days it was impossible for him to get a divorce, even though his wife was flagrantly unfaithful to him. Marian, gravely weighing all factors, decided to defy society and live with Lewes. This made Marian a figure of scandal in London. No "decent" ladies would receive her in their homes (though due to a cruel double standard Lewes was still invited). Only a few radical women and progressive men kept up friendships with Marian. Her family disowned her. In her isolation she depended on Lewes' loyal, protective love. They had decided not to have children (although she soon became a second mother to his sons). Shrewdly, Lewes realized that Marian needed something to engage her emotions as well as her immense intellect. He began to urge her to write fiction.

Self-conscious, afraid of criticism or rejection,

Marian wrote her first story, "Amos Barton," in 1856. Before she would send it to a publisher, however, she and Lewes invented a pen name—George Eliot. She didn't want to publish under her real name, fearing readers would read it only because of her scandalous reputation. She deliberately chose a man's name, too. Many Victorian women wrote novels, but these were often looked down upon as slight, feminine stories. Marian hoped her books would be judged seriously if readers thought a man had written them. (Similarly, a few years earlier, the Brontë sisters had signed male pen names to their novels *Jane Eyre* and *Wuthering Heights*.)

Although George Eliot's first stories were well reviewed, her first full-length novel, *Adam Bede*, was a runaway success. Set in the Warwickshire countryside where Marian had grown up, it vibrated with a simple realism totally new in English literature. No one before had cast ordinary farm laborers as main characters in a novel, or had drawn such complex psychological portraits of them. What's more, the book's plot centered around a farm girl's seduction and her murder of her illegitimate child. Even without Marian Evans' name attached, this was racy stuff.

By 1860, George Eliot was a famous, beloved author. Yet Marian Evans was still a social outcast, and it began to weigh on her. Her first novels sold well, but she and Lewes weren't rich. (He still had to support his wife and her children.) If anything, success only increased the pressure Marian put on herself to write an even better book next time. Although the public loved her realistic stories of English rustic life, Marian was afraid of getting stuck in a rut, and so she planned a new novel set in

Renaissance Italy. But the heavy research it required was bogging her down. Lewes needed to stay in London for his journalistic work. They lived there in a dumpy rented house, surrounded by the gray cityscape. Marian felt cooped up, stifled, cut off from her roots in the country.

Then a vision came to her out of her childhood. It was a picture of an old linen-weaver, with a sad expression on his face, bent under the heavy bag on his shoulder. Floodgates of feeling opened in her. She postponed the Italian novel and began to write *Silas Marner*.

Contemporary readers were delighted with *Silas Marner* because it returned to the rustic characters they'd enjoyed in *Adam Bede*. Yet *Silas Marner* was really a step forward. Behind this simple portrait of country life lies a rigorous examination of the moral forces that drive the universe. Marian believed that writers should not merely entertain the public, but that they had a duty to teach their readers moral truths as well. Having lost her Christian faith, she'd replaced it with a philosophy that kindness, honesty, and courage were necessary for human survival, an ethical code that runs throughout *Silas Marner*. She continued to explore this creed in her later novels, *Felix Holt*, *Middlemarch*, and *Daniel Deronda*.

Eventually, the greatness of George Eliot's work cancelled out her social disgrace. Even Queen Victoria's daughter begged to meet her. Marian and Lewes remained devoted to each other for twenty-five years, and this finally won them as much respect as if they'd been legally married. In fact, after Lewes' death in 1878, when Marian married a much younger man, John Cross, many of her fans were upset. They felt she was being disloyal to Lewes' memory.

In her own time, George Eliot was the most popular author in Britain, more admired even than Dickens, in spite of her notorious personal life. Her literary reputation dipped for several years after her death in 1880, however, as the public taste moved away from long, moralizing novels. Her focus on characters' psychological processes had paved the way for the "modern novel" (both Henry James and Marcel Proust claimed a debt to her), but the experimental fiction of the early twentieth century made her prose style seem old-fashioned. Then one of the chief experimentalists, Virginia Woolf, helped to restore Eliot's reputation. She wrote an essay praising *Middlemarch* as "one of the few books written for adults." Eliot has been considered one of the great writers ever since.

Among her novels, *Silas Marner* is most often chosen for students to read because it is the shortest and, on the surface, the simplest. But it, too, is full of adult wisdom. Though its social philosophies may no longer seem as radical as they did a century ago, this is still an eye-opening, truthful vision of the way the world works.

THE NOVEL

The Plot

Silas Marner, a linen-weaver, works in his solitary cottage by a stone-pit outside the English village of Raveloe. In a flashback, you learn that Marner came to Raveloe fifteen years earlier from a large industrial town where he was part of a fundamentalist Christian sect. But one night, Silas had fallen into a trance while watching over the deathbed of a church elder. Silas' best friend stole a bag of money from the dying man and blamed the theft on Silas. Their sect tried the case by drawing lots, to let God show who was guilty. When this method convicted Silas, he lost his faith in God and soon left the city. Ending up in Raveloe, he kept to himself and worked long hours. Slowly he began to accumulate gold, and this became his one purpose in life.

Godfrey Cass, son of the village squire, at this time needs money. His younger brother Dunstan has borrowed a large sum from Godfrey and now he's lost it. But the money belongs to their father, and Godfrey has to repay it himself. Otherwise Dunstan will tell their father Godfrey's secret—that he's married to a drug-addicted barmaid. Godfrey gives his favorite horse to Dunstan to sell for the money, but Dunstan carelessly kills the horse in a hunting accident. On his way home, Dunstan passes Silas Marner's cottage and sees it empty, with the door open. Walking in, he finds Silas' hoard of gold and steals it, disappearing into the night. When Silas returns home and finds he's been robbed, he is devastated.

Godfrey learns that his horse was found dead. When Dunstan doesn't return, he explains to their father about the money. Squire Cass is angry with Dunstan, but he doesn't probe into why Godfrey lent his shiftless brother the money. He does pressure Godfrey to marry his sweetheart Nancy Lammeter, and Godfrey, still hiding his marriage, hopes somehow he can still marry Nancy.

Though desolated by his loss, Silas is drawn closer to human society by the sympathy of the villagers, especially his neighbor Dolly Winthrop. Dunstan has still not returned home—his family and friends assume he has simply run away. On New Year's Eve, at Squire Cass' annual big party, Nancy Lammeter avoids Godfrey, feeling hurt that he hasn't proposed to her. While he tries to woo Nancy, outside in the snow Godfrey's wife is heading toward the house. She intends to force Godfrey to acknowledge her by appearing at the party with their child. But addiction overcomes her; she takes a dose of opium and passes out in the snow. Her two-year-old daughter wanders off, attracted by the light shining from a nearby cottage. It is Marner's home—he has fallen into another trance and left his door open. When he comes to, he sees the little girl, her hair shining so brightly that at first he thinks his lost gold has magically returned.

After finding the mother in the snow, Silas goes to the Squire's house to fetch the doctor. Recognizing the child in Silas' arms, Godfrey guiltily joins the rescue party, but finding his wife dead, he keeps her identity a secret.

Silas is determined to keep the child, like a treasure he has found. He names her Eppie after his own sister, and he even takes her to church to be christened. His care for Eppie forces him to become part of village life. His love for her changes his personality. As Eppie grows up, Godfrey watches her silently, and occasionally helps Silas out with money. But he doesn't acknowledge her, because now that he's free, he has married Nancy.

Sixteen years pass. Silas and Eppie are happily devoted to each other. Dolly Winthrop's son, Aaron, is Eppie's sweetheart. But at the Cass house, Nancy worries about her marriage. After one stillbirth, she hasn't been able to conceive a child, and Godfrey is wracked with disappointment. He's been urging her to adopt Eppie, but Nancy feels it's against the will of God to adopt a child who is not her own. Then the stone-pit beside Silas' cottage is drained to create new fields. Dunstan's skeleton is discovered at the bottom, clutching Silas' gold. Shaken by the sight, Godfrey tells Nancy the truth about his first marriage. To his surprise, she agrees to adopt Eppie, Godfrey's real daughter.

They go to Marner's cottage with their proposal. Though Silas' gold has been restored to him, he's distraught at the prospect of losing his second, more precious treasure, Eppie. But he lets Eppie make her own choice—and she chooses to stay with Silas. Godfrey and Nancy return home, sad but reconciled. In the spring, Eppie marries Aaron and they walk back to Silas' cottage to live with him.

The Characters

Silas Marner
When she first conceived of the story of Silas Marner, George Eliot thought immediately of one of

her favorite poets, William Wordsworth. He was the first to show country life realistically in poetry, as Eliot was the first in prose fiction. To some degree, Silas Marner is a typical Wordsworthian hero—a simple, instinctual creature, with limited education and imagination, whose life has a natural dignity. But a novel works differently from a poem, and Silas Marner is an unlikely hero for a novel. It isn't just that he's poor, although before George Eliot few authors cast working folk in major roles in novels. It isn't just that he's skinny and pale, with bulging brown eyes—physically unattractive heroes, like Shakespeare's Richard III or Cervantes' Don Quixote, can make powerful literary material. And it isn't just that he's a loner and an alien in Raveloe. Outsiders have made great heroes throughout literature, from Shakespeare's Othello to Emily Brontë's Heathcliff in *Wuthering Heights* to R. P. McMurphy in Kesey's *One Flew Over the Cuckoo's Nest*. These, however, are charismatic, complex personalities. Silas Marner is not. Yet George Eliot gives this simple linen-weaver all the attention most authors save for their most glamorous characters.

Some readers see Silas as a fairy-tale character, like the typical poor old woodcutter who endures poverty and misery in lonely silence for years. In this, he is also like a biblical character, Job. (Silas, however, loses his faith when he is unjustly punished, whereas Job heroically hangs on to his faith while God tests him with rounds of suffering.) Silas simply seems the plaything of some great force guiding the universe, whose plan is inscrutable and maybe even unfair. He's subject to mysterious fits that rob him of his senses for minutes at a time.

The Characters

He does nothing to deserve being expelled from his congregation or having his fiancée Sarah break off their engagement. He does nothing to deserve being robbed fifteen years later by Dunstan Cass. And he does nothing to deserve finding Eppie. These things simply happen to him, like spells or miracles, transforming his life.

This storybook quality is suggested in the book's opening passage, which seems to describe a magical other world. Soon, however, Eliot shifts to a more realistic view. She explains, as an anthropologist might, how superstitious country folk are. She talks about the linen-weavers in sociological terms, as "emigrants from the town into the country." Then you first see Silas in his cottage, weaving away while village boys peer curiously in the windows. He doesn't need to be realistic, some readers argue. The point is that you are asked to fit this eccentric creature into a realistic social context. The villagers see him as a magical figure—they say he works for the devil—but this is a comment on their superstitiousness, not on Silas. As you read, consider how his skills—as a weaver or as a herb-healer—are regarded by the villagers. Watch how his grief over his robbery and his care of Eppie pull him into village life.

Other readers place more emphasis on the passages where Eliot dissects Silas' psychological processes. She explains how he felt when he left Lantern-Yard, how he became a miser, how he reacts to the theft of his gold, how Eppie's presence heals him and draws him back into the mainstream of life. She gives you a medical reason for his fits and shows you how his poor vision often confuses him. In comparison to her analysis of

Godfrey Cass' mind, of course, Silas' psychology seems rudimentary. But those who think Silas is realistic point out that Eliot is trying to portray a limited mind stunted by a poor education and a lifetime of ceaseless work.

The debate over Silas' realism goes on and on. But one thing seems clear—Eliot is sympathetic toward him. She constantly shifts from his perspective to that of the community surrounding him and back again, to show how misunderstood he is. She reminds you that he once had a mother and a sister and a childhood. Silas doesn't act in grand sweeping gestures, but Eliot interprets the strong emotions lying behind his timid little actions. Thus, by the time he makes his meek, stammering appearance at the Rainbow to report his theft, you've already seen him go through an internal agony of disbelief and despair at home. Even though he quietly tells Eppie that she herself must choose between him and her real father, Godfrey, Eliot makes you feel how hard this is for Silas, how devastated he would be if he lost her. Though he is only a simple linen-weaver, she feels his story is worth telling.

Godfrey Cass
Godfrey is in many ways the direct opposite of Silas. He's young, handsome, well-off, and charming. The villagers admire him, even when they suspect he isn't acting right. Unlike Silas, who's alone in the world, Godfrey has too much family—a gruff father, a troublesome brother, a wife and child he doesn't want, and a sweetheart anxiously waiting for him to propose. Silas works hard, but Godfrey has no particular work to do. While Silas

The Characters

endures his exile from society, Godfrey is impatient and a moral coward. Whereas Silas is unjustly punished, time and again Godfrey manages to escape punishment, even for sins he has committed.

Some readers, therefore, see Godfrey as the villain of this novel. His weakness sets Dunstan on a path that ends with Dunstan robbing Silas. While Silas is grieving over his lost gold, Godfrey is relieved because Dunstan has disappeared. He is relieved, too, when his wife Molly is found dead in the snow, because it clears the way for him to marry Nancy Lammeter. At the end of the book, Godfrey selfishly tries to take Eppie away from Silas. But he's finally punished, by Eppie's rejection, for having lied to the world for so many years.

Yet other readers look beyond this formal structure, in which Godfrey plays a villain's role, to judge whether he is really a villainous person. In his first scene, they point out, he appears with his callous brother Dunstan, who makes Godfrey look sensitive and conscientious by comparison. Godfrey seems to know what is right, though he's often too weak to do it. When you see his home environment, you can understand Godfrey's lack of moral fiber. When Eliot traces the tiny mental steps by which he talks himself out of doing the right thing, the process is somehow easy to understand—hasn't everyone rationalized like this at times? His love for Nancy is genuine, and her love for him testifies to something good in his nature. Once they're married, he makes a fine husband, except for his disappointment over their childlessness (which he tries to hide from her). He does have fatherly feelings for Eppie, and he watches her grow up with a constant sense of regret. To these readers, Godfrey is a good but weak man whose fate embodies the moral of the novel.

As you read, for example, the scene on New Year's Eve when Silas appears with the infant Eppie, imagine how other characters judge Godfrey. Just as Eliot gives you special sympathy for Silas, she gives you a special insider's view of Godfrey's weakness. You know his worst impulses—the side that most of us never show to the world. As you read, decide for yourself whether Godfrey is the villain or the tragic hero of this novel.

Nancy Lammeter

For several chapters, you don't actually meet Nancy—you just hear of her as the girl Godfrey wants to marry. She's presented as the proper, socially respectable partner for him, as opposed to his secret wife Molly. Even crude Squire Cass approves of her. Considering what you are shown of the upperclass world she belongs to, how do you feel about Nancy before you meet her?

When Nancy finally appears in Chapter 11, you may be in for a surprise. Eliot enters Nancy's thoughts, to show that she's a gentle, sensitive girl, insecure and confused about Godfrey's courtship. Then you see her through the eyes of the fashionable, town-bred Gunn sisters. They see that she is pretty, well-mannered, and neatly dressed. Nevertheless, she disapproves of their low-cut dresses, and they disapprove of her country dialect—she is clearly part of her country environment. You can see the signs of hard work on Nancy's hands. In general, Eliot describes Nancy's looks and character in glowing terms. Her only faults, Eliot tells you, are a touch of pride and inflexibility.

Having a positive view of Nancy may make you feel more kindly toward the upper class in general (notice that the men at the Rainbow, too, speak well of the Lammeters). It may also give you more sympathy for Godfrey. She seems to be a good influence on him. On the other hand, are her moral standards too high? She keeps Godfrey at arm's length because she's heard bad rumors about him. Even after Molly has died and he is free to marry Nancy, Godfrey is reluctant to tell her about Molly because he fears her disapproval. Later, Nancy's strict code also keeps her from agreeing to adopt a child, which creates the only unhappiness in her marriage to Godfrey. As you read, consider: Is Nancy a good moral example or are her strict principles a flaw in her character?

Dolly Winthrop

Dolly represents Raveloe's values of what an individual should be. She's hardworking, skillful, and so efficient that she has time left over to care for her neighbor Silas. She doesn't hesitate to give advice and get involved with other people's lives. She is motherly, not only toward her own child Aaron but toward Eppie. As a wife, she's tolerant of her husband's drinking but fairly independent. She knows she's no scholar, but she earns great respect from Silas for her ability to see matters clearly, almost instinctively.

Dolly's friendship with Silas demonstrates concretely how the village gradually accepts him. But Dolly serves another function, too—she is the spokesperson for Raveloe religion, holding it up against Silas' Lantern-Yard beliefs. Dolly believes in religion without knowing the fine points of doctrine. While the rituals of the church comfort her, she concentrates on good deeds here on Earth rather than on a relationship with God. Her concept of God is almost pagan, a fuzzy vision of "Them up above." But with true peasant wisdom, she sees a divine pattern in events, working out over long years. She makes Silas look upon his life with this kind of long-range view, showing him that all his sorrows were simply a path leading to his finding Eppie.

Eppie
On the title page of *Silas Marner*, George Eliot placed a quotation from Wordsworth's poem "Michael":

> A child, more than all other gifts
> That earth can offer to declining man,
> Brings hope with it, and forward-looking
>   thoughts.

In the novel, that prophecy is fulfilled by Eppie, the abandoned child that Silas Marner adopts. Symbolically, she is the golden treasure that replaces his stolen gold. Psychologically, she is the force that pulls Silas out of his isolation and restores him to harmony with the human race, as well as with his own past.

Although Eppie fulfills these functions in the novel, she is also an interesting character in her own right. She is believable as a toddler, wandering away from her careless mother toward a shiny light. Her needs are simple—she's hungry and her feet are wet—and she clings lovingly to Silas once he has taken care of these needs. Later, you see her as an active little child, getting into anything that's in her reach.

Pretty Eppie is blonde like her biological father, Godfrey. She's no common village girl, though Eliot says this is the result of her loving environment, not her upperclass blood. In her simple emotions and her strong attachments, Eppie is like her adoptive father, Silas. But she also has unique qualities, associated throughout the novel with animals, flowers, and nature. In the Wordsworth quotation, a child is said to be a gift of Earth—and Eppie is part of that natural bounty.

If Silas is like the poor old woodcutter in a fairy tale, then Eppie is like the woodcutter's daughter—a beautiful, golden-haired girl who's really a princess in disguise. George Eliot turns the fairy tale on its head, though, because this princess doesn't meet a handsome prince. When her real father shows up to offer her a life of riches, she rejects him in favor of the poor old woodcutter. The man she marries is simply a brawny young gardener, Aaron Winthrop, whom she loves more like a brother than a lover. But in this novel's scheme of things, that means she will live happily ever after.

Dunstan Cass

If Godfrey is not the villain of this novel, perhaps his younger brother Dunstan is. Godfrey's sins are all passive—he decides *not* to do something—whereas Dunstan actually commits bad deeds. He squanders the money Godfrey lends him, then he destroys Godfrey's horse while hunting. Finally, he steals Silas' money. What motivates Dunstan? Eliot shows you the twists and turns of his reasoning, just as she does Godfrey's. Both think selfishly, but while Godfrey is aware of moral considerations, Dunstan just calculates what he can get away with. Eliot shows him mostly in upperclass settings, so his vices seem a product of his class. Yet even his own family and friends don't seem to care when Dunstan disappears.

His nickname, Dunsey, sounds like "dunce," and Dunstan doesn't seem very bright. He allows himself to be propelled by circumstances, which he thinks of as "luck." He doesn't plot to rob Silas, but when the opportunity comes his way, he takes it. Soon after, however, he falls into the stone-pit and is drowned. Is this bad luck—or a fitting punishment for his crime?

Squire Cass

In Squire Cass, Eliot embodies what she sees as the worst characteristics of the English gentry—the upper class of country society. He bullies his sons and he patronizes the common people of Raveloe. He's dull-witted and narrow-minded. He isn't hard-working and his pleasures are crude—eating red meat, swilling ale, and making lewd jokes. (Note that his last name sounds like the word "crass.") Squire Cass is a great man in the community because of his hereditary position. The poor never question his wasteful life. But Eliot does, just as she questions the way he has raised his sons. Godfrey wishes his father had disciplined him more. You'll have to decide whether you blame Squire Cass for the tragic events brought about by his wayward sons.

Aaron Winthrop

When Aaron first comes with his mother Dolly to visit Silas, he's still a small child. Silas regards him as an alien creature, but this encounter foreshadows the impact Eppie will have upon Silas. When he's grown up, Aaron becomes Eppie's sweetheart (although she doesn't seem sexually attracted to him). Like Eppie, he is in touch with nature, a gifted gardener. Some readers think Aaron is a cardboard figure, a stereotype of the manly young laborer whom Eppie should choose over a life with Godfrey. Yet others think that his kind, brotherly affection for Eppie represents Eliot's idea of perfect, wholesome love.

Priscilla Lammeter
When blunt-spoken, dumpy Priscilla appears beside her sister Nancy, Nancy's beauty and grace are all the more evident. These sisters show a strong family affection for each other, as the Cass brothers do not. Together with their father, they demonstrate that strong family love does exist in the upper class. Priscilla defines even more strongly than Nancy certain positive traits of the gentry. She is hard-working, practical, and devoted to farming. She doesn't put on upperclass airs. While some readers feel she's too rude and opinionated, others feel that Eliot wanted her that way, to show that, in the country, the leading families may not be as refined as you would expect.

Molly Farren
Godfrey's unfortunate first wife is seen only briefly, in Chapter 12. Up until then she has simply been a nuisance to Godfrey, but now you see her as a living character, struggling through the snow. Her goal is the Red House where she hopes to have her revenge on Godfrey. Yet she seems like a victim herself, rather than a strong avenger. She has

sparks of motherly tenderness, which almost stop her from taking her fatal dose of opium. She is too weak to resist her addiction, however, and soon meets her fate. Is she the victim of her limited background, Godfrey's neglect, and her addiction? Or do you think she, like Godfrey, is morally to blame for taking the easy way out?

The Men At The Rainbow

In classical Greek tragedies, a group of citizens called the Chorus comments upon the action of the main characters. The group of men who meet at the Rainbow serve this function in *Silas Marner*. Their conversation defines the Raveloe values and gives you a sense of how the main characters fit into the society. The scenes of the gentry at the Red House party in Chapter 11 define another part of Raveloe society. But the men from the Rainbow also appear here, as spectators. They are the base of country wisdom that Eliot uses as a moral standard.

This is a fully fleshed-out social group, with a whole range of personalities. There's Dowlas the know-it-all farrier, the sarcastic wheelwright Ben Winthrop, the easy-going butcher Lundy, the old codger Mr. Macey, the deputy clerk Tookey who's the butt of their jokes, and the landlord Mr. Snell who moderates and keeps the peace. Think about groups of people you socialize with—don't they interact in typical roles like this?

Other Elements

SETTING

The opening of *Silas Marner* suggests a world of legend and myth—a pastoral countryside untouched by the modern world, where figures are larger than life. But gradually Eliot establishes that this story occurs in the first years of the nineteenth century, during the Napoleonic wars, when George III was King of England. This is slightly before Eliot's own childhood. It's also before the Reform Act of 1832, which many Englishmen felt marked the end of an era (as Americans today may regard the bombing of Hiroshima or the Vietnam War). It represented for her an age of innocence.

The landscape is the farming country of the English Midlands where George Eliot grew up. The villagers of Raveloe live in isolation only because of their old-fashioned customs—they really aren't that far from the rest of civilization. Upperclass characters, such as the Casses, frequently travel to neighboring towns. In general, the two classes in Raveloe inhabit different worlds. The Rainbow pub is the center of the common folks' world, and Squire Cass' Red House is the center of the gentry's world. The Raveloe gentry are representatives of an ancient British social class—the "squirearchy," well-off rural landowners who wielded local political power and stood independent of the aristocracy. By Eliot's own time, this class had nearly been obliterated. Raveloe's class system is smoothly integrated, however. Upperclass men drink at the Rainbow, too, and villagers are invited to the Red House parties. They all hear the same gossip. Everyone meets at church.

Silas Marner, in contrast, comes from a large industrial town, though he stayed within a smaller community there, his religious sect. While his hometown is a portrait of the "new" industrialized city of the nineteenth century, his sect is a portrait of the fanatical Evangelical or Puritan denominations that had challenged the established Church of England since the sixteenth century. (Eliot herself had briefly been influenced by Evangelicals.) The customs of such a place are totally different from those of Raveloe, so Silas is branded an alien. Therefore, he lives outside the village, in a cottage beside a dangerous, desolate stone-pit. After Eppie enters his life, however, a garden blooms around its walls, signifying the roots he has put down at last.

THEMES

The following are major themes of *Silas Marner*.

1. LUCK AND FATE

Are some people simply luckier than others? Or is there an overall justice ruling life? Different characters in this book answer these questions differently. Dunstan Cass trusts his native good luck, while Godfrey nervously waits to see if his luck will be good or bad. Neither believes in a system of just rewards and punishment, until years later when Godfrey accepts his childlessness as a divine punishment. Dolly Winthrop trusts blindly to the wisdom of "Them" above, but she does believe that good deeds on Earth are fairly rewarded. Silas, however, used to believe in just rewards in his Lantern-Yard days, and his faith was cruelly disappointed. He seems to be the victim of a blind destiny—even Eppie comes to him like a blessing out of nowhere. As you follow this theme through the book, notice its relation to religion (see Theme 2). Consider not only what characters say, but also how their lives eventually work out in the plot.

2. RELIGION

Under the name of Christianity, many different faiths exist in *Silas Marner*. Eliot did not believe in a divine being herself, yet most of her public probably did. How does she present organized religion in this book? On the one hand there is Silas with his joyless, strict Lantern-Yard faith. On the other hand is Dolly with her buoyant, almost pagan Raveloe beliefs. Nancy Lammeter's clear-cut beliefs show how established doctrine can sometimes become too rigid. At times, Eliot implies that religion is no better than superstition. At other times, she sympathetically describes how church rituals comfort the faithful. Religion binds a community like Raveloe together—even Silas feels lost when he breaks with his sect. Yet many readers feel he seems stronger for having lost his faith. He never really regains a belief in God, even after he joins the church in Raveloe. His "redemption" is a product of human, rather than heavenly, love. What does George Eliot seem to propose as the guiding force of the universe?

3. HUMAN AFFECTIONS

What kinds of human ties are important in this novel? There are family ties—weak at the Casses' house but strong for the Lammeters. The bonds of parent and child are especially important, whether they are biological (as with Dolly and Aaron Winthrop) or adoptive (as with Eppie and Silas). When Eppie has to choose between her biological father, Godfrey, and her adoptive father, Silas, what factors count most with her? Wholesome human affections can restore a damaged personality like Silas'. Yet stunted affections, like those at Squire

Cass' house, can damage a basically good person like Godfrey. Look at the way larger communities are bound together, too: Lantern-Yard, the city Silas came from, Raveloe as a whole, or the upper-class society of Raveloe.

4. CHANGE

In Eliot's view, all change is the product of a multitude of tiny factors. The process is so complex that mere humans cannot presume to control it. To examine this theory, Eliot chose for her main setting a community with ingrained old beliefs, a place where change comes slowly. She shows how gradually the collective "mind" of village opinion shifts until it accepts Silas. Many individual characters, too, have fixed habits of thought that are hard to change. Consider, for example, Squire Cass, Nancy Lammeter, old Mr. Macey, Dolly Winthrop, Godfrey's wife Molly, and Silas himself. Choosing a long time span for her story, Eliot shows people changing gradually over the years, as Silas changes before his robbery and then after finding Eppie. She also minutely examines step by step the process of short-term changes—the reasoning that leads Godfrey to keep his secret marriage hidden or that makes Dunstan rob Silas.

5. THE IMPORTANCE OF THE PAST

Raveloe is a society strongly connected to its past. In contrast, the town Silas comes from seems impersonal and transient—when Silas returns thirty-two years later, Lantern-Yard has been literally wiped off the face of the Earth. Individuals in this book also are connected to their own pasts in different degrees. Godfrey hopes to bury his past. Silas and Eppie cherish their past together. As Silas is redeemed by his love for Eppie, he regains a sense of his past, and memory heals him. Attachment to the past can be stultifying, however, for characters like Squire Cass and Nancy Lammeter. Look at the role played in this novel by local traditions, personal memories, and familiar objects or places. By her own comments, then, Eliot gives this story, set in the past, a meaning for her own modern world.

6. OTHER THEMES

In *Silas Marner*, Eliot also examines the **class system** of England in microcosm (mark the differences between the upper and lower classes, and judge Eliot's comments on them). Connected to this is her belief in **the importance of work.** The villagers understand the value of having a craft or skill and the role this gives one in a community. Silas clings to his craft when all else is taken from him. In the upper class, the Lammeter girls understand hard work, but the Cass sons are dangerously idle. In examining the social structure of Raveloe, however, Eliot **defines a society that no longer exists.** In describing Raveloe—particularly by comparing it to the town Silas comes from—she depicts an England that may have been destroyed by the spread of the Industrial Revolution.

STYLE

At her best, George Eliot writes in a strong, precise style, each word chosen carefully. At her worst, her sentences circle around what she's trying to say, stringing out clauses loaded with abstract, colorless words. In the second paragraph of the book, for example, she starts off with a plain sentence that sets up Silas' situation in simple, concrete words. But by the end of the paragraph she's tangled up in long, meandering sentences, using abstract terms like "a shadowy conception of power that by much persuasion can be induced to refrain from inflicting harm." This puts some readers off before they've even gotten into the book.

When George Eliot is not speaking to the reader directly, however, her style is less self-conscious. Often she takes on the voice of a village gossip to show the community's view of Silas; her language becomes casual, humorous, and colloquial. (See for example the fifth sentence in that second paragraph, beginning "They had, perhaps, heard their mothers and fathers hint. . . .") When she takes on the voice of an upperclass observer, she uses a light, arch irony. (See the first paragraph of Chapter 3.) Her scenes of straight dialogue can also be surprisingly dramatic, as characters use distinctive dialects, and speeches move energetically back and forth.

Woven into the structure of the novel is a complex and subtle web of symbols. Eliot doesn't point them out—you have to be on the lookout for them. She uses imagery drawn from nature to show that human life follows the same laws as the rest of the organic world. She compares Silas to insects, and she shows his love for Eppie growing like a plant. Habits of thought are described as flowing streams. Symbols are not always used as metaphors, however. For example, Eliot frequently mentions the gentry's horses. These are real animals in the story, but they symbolize the gentry's world whenever they appear. Similarly, Silas' gold coins become associated with Eppie's golden hair, symbolizing that both are precious to Silas. Another important strand of imagery is the opposition of light and dark. But as you trace it through the book, be careful—the meanings of George Eliot's symbols shift and change. Her moral vision is too complex to be set out like an allegory, where symbols represent abstract concepts in clear-cut patterns. Instead, her symbols are like little hidden signs, enriching the message you draw from the plot.

POINT OF VIEW

Technically, *Silas Marner* has an omniscient third-person narrator—a narrator who isn't a character but can enter the thoughts and sensations of all the characters. This lets George Eliot delve into her characters' psychological processes, to show the mind of Godfrey, as well as Silas, and then to contrast them. Dunstan's and Nancy's minds are probed, too. With the rest of her characters, however, who provide a social context for the story, the narrator steps back and adopts the role of a social observer. She analyzes the patterns of village life and comments on them—often with the perspective of someone from the outer world.

Maybe that's why it isn't quite true to say that George Eliot is not a character in her novels. She isn't a figure acting in the plot, but her presence certainly is felt as she speaks to the reader. (At the end of the second paragraph, notice that she uses the first person.) Her commentaries bridge the gap between Raveloe and your world. Sometimes she needs to explain attitudes and ideas that would seem strange to "modern" readers. (There's a lot of this in the first chapter.) Sometimes she shows you parallels between the events of the story and your own life. (Look, for example, at Chapter 2, where she compares Silas' hoarding to the way sophisticated men bury themselves in their work.) These comments keep you from getting too caught up in the story. But this is intentional—Eliot wants you always to think about the moral significance of what is happening. Some readers resent this preaching and feel that the story itself teaches the lesson well enough without her comments. Yet other people enjoy her interpreting remarks, feeling that they open up depths of wisdom in this seemingly simple novel.

FORM AND STRUCTURE

Silas Marner is divided into Part One and Part Two, separated by sixteen years in time. The flashback in Chapter 1 travels an equal sixteen years in time, creating a fundamental symmetry (see diagram on page 29). Some readers have felt that the gap between the two parts is too long—they would like to watch Silas being transformed by his love for Eppie, not just be told about it. Yet in Chapter 14 Eliot does show the first stages of the process in detail, and in Chapter 16 she backtracks to fill in even more.

This novel is divided into two parts in another, more important way. While Silas follows a cycle from misery back to happiness, Godfrey Cass follows an opposite path, from a life rich with possibilities to an unfulfilled existence. (See the diagram.) Eliot shifts back and forth between these two plots continually. Silas and Godfrey rarely meet face to face, yet they are linked—through Dunstan, who cheats Godfrey and robs Silas, and later through Eppie, whom Godfrey abandons and Silas adopts.

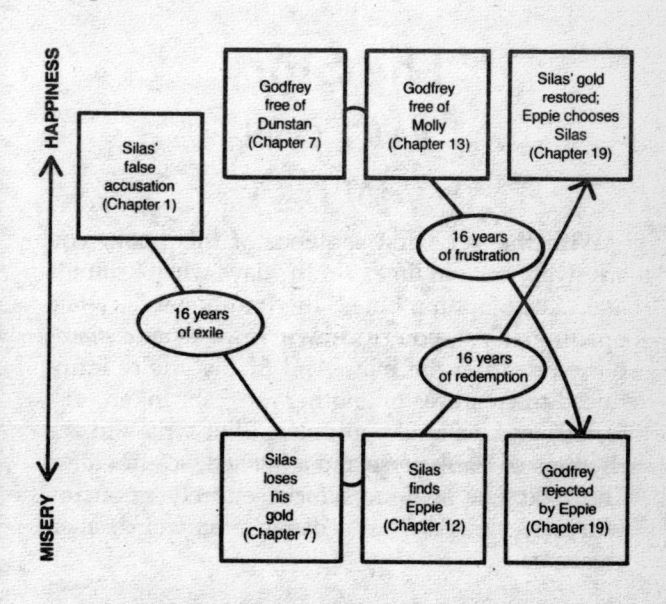

HAPPINESS ↑

- Silas' false accusation (Chapter 1)
- Godfrey free of Dunstan (Chapter 7)
- Godfrey free of Molly (Chapter 13)
- Silas' gold restored; Eppie chooses Silas (Chapter 19)

16 years of exile

16 years of frustration

16 years of redemption

- Silas loses his gold (Chapter 7)
- Silas finds Eppie (Chapter 12)
- Godfrey rejected by Eppie (Chapter 19)

↓ MISERY

Some readers feel the novel is split in two, that Silas' half is like a simple folktale with its happy ending, while Godfrey's half is a complex psychological study with a sad, realistic conclusion. Other readers say that the two halves are separated by different moral climates. In Silas' story, fate is ruled by mysterious pagan gods. Human beings can only surrender themselves and trust these inscrutable divinities. Godfrey's story is like a stern Greek tragedy, where a man's own actions lead inexorably to a tragic climax. Pain and suffering are necessary for him to purge himself of his sin.

To counteract this split, Eliot's elaborate system of parallels, contrasts, and symmetries holds the two stories together.

The Story

PART ONE

CHAPTER 1

With the very first sentence of this book, you are swept back in time. "In the days when" sounds like "Once upon a time," the traditional fairy-tale opening. Next you're drawn to a distant place, buried deep in the hills. And finally you're introduced to creatures of another race, shrunken, distorted, and pale, like gnomes. Eliot writes in the rhythms of blank verse and a hushed, solemn tone. The next few sentences focus entirely upon the weavers, viewed from a distance as weird, alien creatures.

NOTE: Eliot was inspired to write this novel by a memory of a weaver she had seen in her childhood. The dominant features she remembered were the bag on his back, his stooped shoulders, and an "expression of face that led her to think he was an alien from his fellows," according to her publisher John Blackwood. Look at this figure silhouetted against the sky—solitary, sad, and weighed

Chapter 1

down. It's a strong visual image, which would make a striking opening shot of a movie.

Because the weavers come from another part of the country, villagers see them as a threat and shun them. Eliot asks you to understand the mentality of people who have no contact with the world outside their home village. In Eliot's time, this was already hard for readers to grasp. Just think how much harder it is for us, living in our mobile society of supersonic jets, long-distance telephones, satellite television, and space shuttles! Try, however, to put yourself into the villagers' frame of mind for a minute, and imagine how you would regard the lone figure of the weaver.

Now, after the broad sweeping opening, Eliot moves from the general to the particular—to one weaver named Silas Marner. She shows you the precise location of his cottage and makes you hear the rasping sound of his loom. Some readers have pointed out that Silas is unlike the villagers because he works with a machine. Others point out that the farmers work with machines, too—Eliot mentions the winnowing-machine and flail—but those sounds are familiar to Raveloers, while the loom's sound is not. The loom does seem to have taken over Silas' spirit. As the lively village boys peer in the window, you see Silas bent like a slave at his work, unaware of the world around him.

Notice how Eliot shifts in and out of different minds. One moment she is with the boys, looking in the window. The next moment, she sympathizes with harmless Silas, irritated at the interruption. Then she shares the boys' terror as they run from Silas' goggle-eyed stare. She moves from there into the minds of their parents, with their primitive superstitions.

NOTE: Author's comments Eliot pauses to discuss this superstitious quality of the peasant mind. In her sociological analysis, however, her language becomes abstract and incomprehensible. What she's really saying is that the peasants' life is hard, so they naturally think God is harsh, too. It's interesting that Eliot refers to her own experience with an old laborer to illustrate this concept. It's as if she's proving her credentials as a social analyst.

Now Eliot fills in the details of her setting. She locates Raveloe on the map, in the English Midlands. She sets a date for the story, by referring to coach-roads (by Eliot's own day, railroads had replaced coaches) and the Napoleonic Wars. She describes the buildings of the village and sketches its social hierarchy, headed by a few farmers with large land holdings. Picture the village to yourself. Do you think it's a glorified vision or a realistic one? What evidence can you point to?

Silas came to this place from the north fifteen years ago, you learn, but he's never joined in the village life. Eliot shows you the villagers' view of him. She tells Jem Rodney's story about finding Silas in a paralyzed trance on the road one day, and you overhear the locals' eager discussion about this event. The gossipers also refer to another incident, when Silas magically used herbs to cure someone named Sally Oates. After this, Eliot ex-

Chapter 1

plains in her own voice why Marner is tolerated in Raveloe—they fear him and, pragmatically, they need his skill.

Then she plunges deeper, into Silas' past. She speaks of his "metamorphosis"—a scientific word for an insect's change in shape. (Watch for more insect imagery.) Indeed, you learn, he was a different creature in the past. He was deeply involved in a small religious sect, made up mostly of skilled workers like himself. Unlike the villagers, these people thought Silas' trances were a sign of God's favor. Silas also had a dear best friend, William Dane. Dane, however, with his narrow eyes and egotism, forms a definite contrast to Silas, with his deer-like eyes and his gentle, trusting nature.

NOTE: Eliot seems unsympathetic to the Lantern-Yard sect. The very name suggests that its faith casts only a dim light (a lantern) of knowledge in a closed-in space (a yard). She says that it gives its members a sense of security, but she describes their joyless beliefs with heavy irony. Notice how long and roundabout her sentences get, mocking the brethren's interpretation of Silas' fits. She also shows how they persuaded Silas to give up his herbal studies, which he enjoyed. Her description of Dane's views is sarcastic, while she pities Silas for his earnest doubts.

Eliot continually hints at William's falseness as she tells Silas' story. Dane seems to undermine Silas' engagement to Sarah and his place in the sect (Dane interprets Silas' fits as a mark of the devil).

So when you see Silas sharing with William the job of nursing an ill deacon of the church, you may suspect trouble. Silas stays late at the old man's bedside, but William never shows up. Silas falls asleep—or probably has a fit—and when he comes to, the deacon is dead. Silas innocently goes off to work as usual. But that night he is summoned to a mysterious church meeting (it's William Dane who comes to fetch him). There, Silas is shown his own pocket-knife, which was found in the dead deacon's dresser drawer—where a bag of church money should have been.

Silas, knowing he's innocent, stays calm. But when the brethren search his house, William finds the money (he probably hid it there). While William is accusing him, Silas remembers with a sickening jolt that William had borrowed his knife the day before, but loyally he says nothing. The congregation tries the case by praying and drawing lots.

NOTE: Lots This, Eliot says, was typical practice for some sects. They bypassed the legal process, believing that only God should judge and punish offenders. In this ritual, everyone in the group drew a slip of paper. Whoever drew a particular marked slip was judged guilty. William Dane probably fixed it so Silas would draw the damning piece of paper.

Silas feels sure he'll be cleared, although he's already disturbed by William's treachery. Then comes the shocking decision—the lots show that Silas is guilty. What could he have done to prove his innocence? What would you have done in his place? He is asked to leave the sect, to return the money, and to confess his guilt. He protests, explaining that William had the knife. But in the heat of emotion, he speaks against God, causing the brethren to side with William. Silas leaves with his faith in God as shattered as his faith in his fellow man.

Silas' reaction is extreme, for his world has been turned upside down. He seems helpless and passive. He doesn't try to regain Sarah's confidence, he doesn't question the church's decision—he just buries himself in his familiar, repetitive work. As you might expect, Sarah soon marries William Dane. Silas leaves town so quietly that the brethren don't know about it until he's gone.

CHAPTER 2

Imagine setting foot on another planet, with a moonlit rocky landscape and a green sky. Imagine trying to talk to the natives—purple blobs of flesh that emit high-pitched whines. You might feel the way Silas Marner does when he arrives in Raveloe. Its landscape is unfamiliar—woods instead of rolling hills—and its people are slow-moving and prosperous, totally unlike the urban artisans he's lived among. Eliot stresses that this shock would have fallen especially hard on a simple mind like Silas'. His thoughts fly back longingly to Lantern-Yard, picturing the chapel and hearing the familiar service again. Though he has broken with its doctrines, he's still tied in his heart to the physical place, from years of association. This is natural, Eliot tells you—and she compares him to a child, responding instinctively to a parent's sheltering care. Already Eliot is foreshadowing the attachment to Eppie which will be his salvation.

Eliot looks back in time, comparing Silas' faith to some ancient religion, ruled by local gods who co-existed easily with their neighbors' gods. In Eliot's own time, people debated endlessly over which religious group truly represented the universal God. Eliot, however, thought there should be room on Earth for many different religions.

NOTE: Light/dark imagery At the end of this second paragraph, light stands for knowledge and darkness stands for uncertainty. Right now Silas is frightened by life's mysteries—"the blackness of night." This image recurs at the end of the next paragraph, too, in his "dark" future. Yet in the paragraph after that, when he receives his first gold coins, their "brightness" seems simply to mean they're desirable.

Eliot the psychologist reveals how young Silas Marner turns into that bent old man you saw earlier. First, he takes refuge in his work. Eliot compares him to a lower life form, a spider (insect imagery), especially apt because like a spider Silas weaves a web. Eliot says it's normal for any person to bury himself in work when life isn't going well. If you've ever known any workaholics, you may understand this defense.

Silas' life is reduced to a series of physical actions—throwing the shuttle, watching the cloth grow, preparing meals. He doesn't allow himself to reflect upon his past, present, or future. Notice the image used to describe his worn channel of thought—"its old narrow pathway."

One day, a Mrs. Osgood pays Silas in gold for the linen he weaves for her. Although Silas has no purpose for the coins, he likes them for physical reasons—they feel and look good. His old Puritan work ethic becomes transformed into a desire for the money itself. The new feeling grows like a plant, rooted in old feelings (here is another major strand of imagery).

Now you learn the full story of Silas' curing Sally Oates. Though he's trying to shut off memory, when he sees the sick cobbler's wife he remembers how the same disease killed his mother. The memory of his mother reminds him of his herbal medicines, and he treats Sally. In a place like Raveloe, however, there are few private deeds. Soon everyone wants some of Silas' "stuff." Being honest, Silas doesn't claim any special powers, but when he refuses to treat other people, the villagers turn against him more than ever. Eliot notes ironically that this deed, which might have forged human ties for him, only drove him farther away.

As Silas' coins begin to pile up, he becomes obsessed with accumulating more. He hides them in a hole in the floor, which Eliot shows you precisely. She explains that there's little robbery in Raveloe, however—everyone would recognize the stolen objects if the thief used them. Some readers believe here that Silas feels his loom and his coins are alive. But others are quick to point out that in the next paragraph, Eliot says he becomes harder, narrower, and bent, until he has a "mechanical relation to the objects of his life." Do you think Silas is a machine? Consider this as you read on.

One day, however, Silas drops an old brown pot

that he's used for years. The familiar object felt like a real living thing to him. He grieves when it breaks, and he carries the pieces home to keep on a shelf. Notice Eliot's simple language here—what kind of an effect does it create?

Before the chapter ends, Eliot gives you another detailed picture of Silas, weaving all day, caressing his coins at night. Once again, he ignores the herbs in the fields for his new "religion" of gold. Notice repeated imagery—the coins are like "unborn children" (another foreshadowing of Eppie) and his life has dwindled to one narrow channel of thought. (Literally, he never walks off the path on his daily journeys. Metaphorically, his life has become like a dried-up rivulet, trickling through the sand.) But now that Silas' metamorphosis is complete, Eliot tells you, an event is coming to change his life.

CHAPTER 3

Eliot leaves you in suspense about Silas' great change while she shifts to the other end of the social spectrum. Squire Cass is the greatest man in Raveloe, she tells you, although her tone is ironic. She first discusses the local gentry as villagers might—pointing out Cass' big brick house, casually mentioning the Osgoods. But then she discusses these landowners with an outsider's perspective. She makes you aware that political conditions later brought this class to ruin, through their wasteful living habits and poor farming. Yet when she describes the generous feasts that people like Cass and Osgood hold, she paints a glowing picture of old-fashioned plenty. (You'll see one of these feasts later, in Chapter 11.) The poor enjoy this bounty, too. Do you think Eliot approves or disapproves of this social system? What evidence supports your opinion?

There's a reason why Squire Cass throws big raucous parties and spends his time at the local pub—his wife died long ago. Eliot expresses here her ideal of woman's role—as a source of order, refinement, and loving feelings. Lacking a mother, the Cass sons have turned out badly. Compare this all-male family to Silas Marner's, which seems to consist only of himself, a mother, and a sister.

Eliot lets you hear the village gossip about Dunstan and Godfrey. While Dunstan sounds thoroughly bad, Godfrey seems good-hearted. But people have been worried about Godfrey's behavior lately. Everyone's hoping he'll straighten himself out by marrying Nancy Lammeter, obviously the daughter of another important Raveloe family.

Now you meet the Cass brothers in person, so you can make up your own mind about them. As Godfrey stands by the fire, the parlor around him defines his gloomy mood. It's dimly lit and messy, full of pleasure's leftovers—discarded hunting clothes, half-empty mugs of beer, ashy pipes, and a dying fire. When Dunsey, who's been drinking, strolls into the room, his jeering tone lives up to the villagers' opinion of him. Agitated, Godfrey demands that Dunstan return the money he borrowed from Godfrey, which was a tenant's rent payment. Dunstan knows how to manipulate Godfrey, though. He threatens to tell the Squire about Godfrey's marriage to drunken Molly Farren, and Godfrey reacts with fear. Now you know why lately Godfrey's been acting strangely.

> **NOTE: Parallels** Like Silas, Godfrey is taken advantage of by a thieving brother. (Dane was like a brother to Silas.) Both hope to marry a nice young woman but are prevented by shameful situations—Silas' conviction and Godfrey's marriage. What obvious contrasts, however, can you point to?

This is the first scene Eliot dramatizes directly. She doesn't comment much, except to show characters' gestures and expressions. In slangy, lively speech, the brothers refer casually to people they know, whom you haven't met. You've caught them in the midst of life, with upcoming events (the hunt, Mrs. Osgood's party) and ongoing quarrels. Afraid of their father, they blackmail each other. Godfrey declares he may confess his marriage to the Squire to shake off Dunstan's hold on him. But Eliot takes you into his thoughts, to show that this springs from desperation more than courage—Molly's been threatening to reveal herself to his father, anyway. He thinks over the consequences of confession: losing Nancy and being disinherited. Bred to a useless life, he couldn't do anything for a living. Dunstan knows how to handle his brother. He sits back, waiting until Godfrey has cowardly talked himself out of this move.

Godfrey realizes that he must sell his horse Wildfire to get the money. Actually, this is Dunstan's suggestion, and Dunstan convinces his flustered brother to let him sell the animal. Compare Dunstan's cool confidence in his own luck to Godfrey's nervous decision to risk getting caught rather than turn himself in. Which brother seems the

Chapter 3

stronger in this scene? Which brother do you like better? Why?

After Dunstan has left, Eliot enters Godfrey's thoughts with sympathetic insight into his problems. Surprisingly, even though Godfrey is from the top rung of rural society, Eliot says he lacks culture. Typically, she tangles herself up in a long, indirect, abstract sentence to express this. ("The subtle and varied pains springing of the higher sensibility . . . that dreary absence of impersonal enjoyment and consolation . . . the perpetual urgent companionship of their own griefs and discontents.") In the last chapter, she asked you to pity how Silas' simple mind reacted to his situation. Here, she urges you to feel sorry for Godfrey because even a crude squire's son feels pain when his life turns out badly.

Next Eliot explains how Godfrey got into this jam—Dunstan urged him on in his brief passion for Molly. But Godfrey doesn't feel like a victim, as Silas did. He knows his own foolish bad habits are to blame, though it's agonizing knowledge. In contrast to this, his love for Nancy summons the better side of his nature, the side that's muffled in his motherless home. Read this passage carefully. Do you think Eliot blames him or excuses him for his mistakes?

Either way, Eliot tells you, Godfrey's too weak to face up to his position. He's willing to let Dunstan sell his horse for him. That way he can go to a party where he'll see Nancy, and avoid the town where Molly lives. After all his soul-searching, he lets his mind slide back into bad habits and heads for the pub. Eliot shows his growing hardness as he pushes his dog aside. The dog follows him, however, because she's too dumb to assert herself—just like Godfrey.

CHAPTER 4

You enter Dunstan's thoughts as he rides Wildfire to the hunt the next morning. Passing Silas' cottage, he remembers village rumors about the weaver's hoard of money and considers getting Godfrey to borrow money from Silas. These are idle thoughts, such as you might have about anybody when you drive past that person's house. Nevertheless, Eliot told you at the end of Chapter 2 that a change was coming in Silas' life, so now you should be on guard. Dunstan doesn't think the plan through, but the idea is planted in his mind. He decides to go on and sell Wildfire, though, for the fun of horse-trading and of hurting Godfrey. Notice that Dunstan's motives are all negative. At the hunt, he lies for the sake of lying. The other men, Bryce and Keating, however, understand what Dunstan's up to—they don't seem any better than he is. Maybe his vices are typical of this social class. Do you think Dunsey's an interesting villain? Why?

Dunstan wangles a high price for the horse, as he expected. But this good luck goes to his head. He doesn't do the sensible thing, which would be to deliver the horse safely right away. Instead, he takes Wildfire on the hunt. When he falls behind the other hunters, he rides recklessly. He pushes the horse to jump over a hedge, and Wildfire falls onto a sharp stake. The horse is killed, yet Dunstan doesn't even seem upset about this accident—he's just glad that no one was watching. He doesn't

Chapter 4

reflect that his luck has turned bad, or that he's to blame. All of his reasoning centers on what he can do next. He figures Godfrey won't be too angry because Dunstan has another plan—borrowing money from Silas—to offer him. He'd like to rent another horse to ride home, but since he hasn't got enough money, he convinces himself that it's a shorter route to go straight home. With a cocky air, he sets off, thinking about how he'll make people at the pub admire him when he boasts of how he walked all the way home.

NOTE: Weather Notice the mist gathering here. It may remind you of scenes in movies in which swirling mist creates a sense of imminent danger. The mist in this chapter, however, also symbolizes Dunstan's confused sense of right and wrong. Eliot often uses weather to express a moral environment. This chapter, for example, started on a cold, wet morning, attuned to Dunstan's malicious mind. Watch the role that weather plays as the story moves on.

Typically, Dunstan still thinks he's a lucky fellow, just because he's getting home without being seen. Yet he's surrounded by mist, rain, and darkness, and he stumbles along the road until a light shines out. (Note the darkness and light imagery again.) He realizes that it's Silas' cottage. Dunsey's half-baked plan for borrowing money from Silas has been growing in his dim mind as he walked. He decides to get started on it right now.

Dunstan is surprised that the old weaver isn't

home and that his door's unlocked. The brightness and warmth inside are inviting, though, so Dunstan walks in and makes himself at home. Dunstan, with upperclass prejudice, is surprised that Silas has pork roasting for dinner. Of course, this *is* out of character for Silas' reputation as a miser, but most poor folks back then couldn't afford meat more than once a week. Remember this when you see how the gentry eat.

Eliot traces Dunstan's thinking step by step. He notices the pork roasting slowly, hung over the fire from a string attached to a door-key. Silas obviously has stepped out only for a moment. Dunstan thinks of the nearby stone-pit and leaps to the conclusion that Silas has fallen in. That would make it easy for him to steal the old man's money. This is such an attractive idea that he assumes Silas is dead and starts to wonder where the money is. Dunstan can only think of obvious hiding places, but Silas has chosen an obvious one. Dunstan notices a spot in the floor where the sand has been moved around. (People scattered sand over their floors to absorb dirt back then.) He pries up the bricks to find Silas' two bags of gold.

Look at how easy, almost accidental, this theft is. The money seems to fall into Dunstan's hands. Some readers see this as a sign of fate—that Dunstan was meant to steal Silas' gold for some divine purpose. Others see it as a sign that life is random, and that Silas is still a victim.

Dunstan seems a little confused by this opportunity, but he doesn't stop to think clearly. He scoops up the gold, replaces the bricks, and slips outside. The darkness of night seems to be his element, now—he seeks refuge in it. Is this another case of Dunstan's good luck? Wait and see how things turn out.

CHAPTER 5

There's a sharp contrast as Eliot switches to a picture of Silas, trudging along the road. He looks pathetic, huddled under a sack against the rain, but unlike Dunstan his mind is at ease. Eliot finds this ironic—the deed that will devastate him is already done.

NOTE: Author's comment Eliot digresses to discuss how people fool themselves into feeling secure. She says they follow a "logic of habit"—you feel safe only because you've been safe for years. After a long convoluted sentence explaining this in the abstract, she gives examples from everyday life. What tone of voice do you hear her using here?

Silas innocently looks forward to his hot dinner. You learn that Dunstan was right—it's unusual for Silas to have meat for dinner. Miss Priscilla Lammeter (Nancy's sister, you might guess) gave it to him. Silas' thoughts explain why his door wasn't locked: the key was part of his rig for roasting his meat, and when he remembered a last-minute errand, it was too much trouble to take it down. Eliot describes the chain of events carefully, showing how each decision—unimportant in itself—led to the robbery. In your opinion, does this make Silas responsible for what happens to him?

Try to see the next scene through Silas' blurry,

nearsighted vision. Entering his cottage, he sees nothing unusual. The fire blazes as he moves around the room, putting his lantern, hat, and sack in their usual places. Meanwhile, you can see what he doesn't see—two sets of footprints in the sand. As he adjusts the meat and settles near the warm hearth, you view his face, lit by the fire. You see him as the villagers do—skinny, bug-eyed, and pale. But then Eliot takes you inside his soul, repeating what she's pointed out before—that he clung to his monotonous loom and hard gold only because his faith had deserted him.

Silas decides to give himself his nightly pleasure of looking at his gold. Watch the shifting value of gold in this chapter. Eliot says it is hard, making Silas' soul hard. Yet the coins' effect on Silas is also like wine, bringing intoxicated joy. Later, when he realizes his gold is gone, he thinks of it as another human who's abandoned him.

He doesn't notice anything out of place at first as he opens the hiding place. His heart thumps wildly when he sees the hole empty, but the idea that the gold is really gone doesn't register all at once. Have you ever lost or broken something valuable? If so, you may understand this sense of stunned disbelief.

Watch how Silas' actions, like an actor's in a play, express the stages of his panic and grief. He gropes around the hole again and again, until he's trembling so hard he nearly drops his candle. Then he searches his entire cottage, turning things inside out, hoping that maybe he'd put the bags somewhere different for a change. He feels around the hole again. He rocks back, looks feverishly around the room, and then puts his hands to his head and cries out. Finally, he staggers over to sit at his loom, the one comfort he has left.

Silas tries to think clearly. He focuses on the idea of a thief, because he might get the gold back from a thief. Reasoning that his money had to have been taken that night, he searches outside in the rain and mud for footprints. For a moment, his hysteria surfaces and he fears a supernatural power at work—the same one that struck him down before—but he pushes that thought away and returns to the idea of a thief. Naturally, he suspects people from the village and seizes upon one man, Jem Rodney, as the probable thief. (Remember Jem Rodney—the poacher who discovered Silas having a fit once by the roadside?) Because it relieves his mind, Silas invents evidence pointing to Jem. Eager for action, he runs out into the rain to summon the authorities. He doesn't lock his door—there's nothing to protect anymore.

Eliot moves out of Silas' limited, intense emotional state to the more relaxed world of the village. She conveys Marner's opinion of the Rainbow—a sinful place (his moral judgment is still Puritan) for the husbands of his customers. But it's where the authorities are likely to be, so that's where he heads.

NOTE: Eliot explains the social hierarchy of the pub. The richer customers drink in one room, the parlor, while commoners gather across the hall in the kitchen. (Many English pubs today still have a refined saloon bar and a plainer public bar.) At the Rainbow, the gentlemen drink hard liquor—"spirits"—while poor men drink cheap beer. The people of Raveloe seem to like this stratification. It is fluid, though. Tonight, for example, the richest gentry are away at the Osgoods' party. Therefore, the lower upperclass men who weren't invited have moved over to the lowerclass bar, where they can be the big shots. Does this seem confusing to you? If so, just think of how a stranger would react to the different cliques and social categories in your school.

CHAPTER 6

Eliot backtracks to recount the evening's conversation at the Rainbow. This re-establishes your sense of the Raveloe community, which contrasts against Silas' isolated existence.

NOTE: Dutch Realism If you could paint Eliot's description of the men at the pub, it would probably look like a seventeenth-century Dutch painting by Jan Vermeer or Frans Hals. Eliot admired this school of art, called "genre" painting, which featured tavern or kitchen scenes in realistic detail. You can see here figures side-lit by the fire, and pipe-smoke hanging in the air. Facial expressions are drawn dramatically. Social distinctions are clear in details of drink and clothing.

There isn't anything important these men have to say—they talk for the sake of fellowship. Mr. Snell, the landlord, like a master of ceremonies,

Chapter 6

begins the conversation by speaking to his cousin the butcher. As you read this scene, be aware of how slow it is, full of long pauses, repetitions, and rambling arguments. Today, people talk quickly, getting right to the point, and jump from topic to topic. But in an old society like Raveloe's, people took all night to speak their minds.

The butcher and the farrier (blacksmith) get into an argument over the breed of a slaughtered cow. The farrier likes arguing for the sake of it, but he can't get the easygoing butcher to fight. Mr. Snell ends this pig-headed quarrel and shifts the topic to the Lammeter family, who owned the cow. He calls on the parish-clerk Mr. Macey, who sparks another quarrel with his new deputy Mr. Tookey. In this ongoing dispute, not only do Macey and Tookey know exactly what they're arguing about, others such as the wheelwright Ben Winthrop butt in, too. The whole community cares about how Tookey does his job. They also care about music and the ritual of the church service.

Originally, George Eliot wanted to write *Silas Marner* in verse. (You can be glad she didn't—her poetry was usually stilted and boring.) She changed to prose because she felt the story would need humor. This chapter demonstrates the kind of humor she meant—based on funny personalities rather than wisecracks. Part of you may be laughing *at* these yokels, like the pompous farrier with his thickheaded arguments. But another part of you may laugh *with* them—at the interplay of characters, the teasing banter, and the droll understatements, like Mr. Macey's comment that there are two opinions about every man. The ribbing is good-natured (notice how out-of-place Ben Winthrop's harsh insults sound) and someone like Mr. Snell always restores harmony.

NOTE: Dialect Although everyone in Raveloe probably spoke with a country accent, Eliot distinguishes the lower classes by writing their speeches in dialect. This was unusual in Victorian novels, although Shakespeare's comic "rustic scenes" provided a model for her. Eliot's dialect is just thick enough to give you the flavor of a rural world. Notice the several techniques she uses. She spells a word as it is pronounced ("allays," "nat'ral"). She uses ungrammatical constructions ("it's no better nor a hollow stalk"). She has her characters use countrified sayings ("I'd keep him in liver and lights for nothing"). Occasionally she uses unusual dialect words ("throstle").

Snell smoothes everyone's feelings and then prods Mr. Macey once more to tell his story about Mr. Lammeter. This story's been told many times before—probably in the same words—but everyone enjoys hearing it again. It's like hearing your favorite comedian do a routine that you know by heart.

Eliot wrote this long anecdote for another reason—to show how people in Raveloe regard aliens. The first Mr. Lammeter, like Silas, came from the outside world, which to Raveloers seems like another planet. But Mr. Lammeter fit in with their values. He brought good sheep with him, and he "know'd the rights and customs o' things." As

Macey traces the Lammeter family tree, you see how much these people feel connected with the past.

Mr. Macey finally tells his story about the Lammeters' wedding, when the minister that day mixed up the questions and responses in the ceremony. Mr. Macey was afraid the marriage wouldn't be legal. (Note how outward forms and rituals are important.) The minister, however, being an authority figure, set Macey's mind at ease.

The next story Macey tells is in direct contrast. Another outsider, a man named Cliff from London, owned the Warrens before the Lammeters. Though he was a tailor, he tried to move into the upper class (notice how horses symbolize the upper class here). Not only did Cliff violate the Raveloe class system, he also rejected the dignity of his trade.

One more element of the Raveloe mind surfaces in this story—superstition. Cliff was rumored to have a relationship with the Devil (much as Silas is supposed to). The men argue over whether the Warrens' stables are haunted. Not everyone in the pub believes in ghosts—the farrier, Mr. Dowlas, is as you'd expect a skeptic. But this lively debate suggests that plenty of people in Raveloe do believe in ghosts. Belligerently, the farrier dares any ghost to come stand inside. At this moment, Silas walks in.

CHAPTER 7

At first you see Silas as the men at the Rainbow see him—a weird figure who doesn't fit in the convivial surroundings. Eliot gently mocks their reaction to Silas, using insect imagery again, in their curious quivering antennae. Their minds still running on ghosts, the men look at him as if he were one. Then Mr. Snell, as the host, addresses Silas. Silas replies in broken, agitated phrases, calling for the authorities. He injects a note of tragedy into this comic evening.

The men don't react to the news of his robbery at first. When Silas accuses Jem Rodney, Jem seems more annoyed than afraid. Jem's one of the poorer customers, sitting far from the fire, yet he is more accepted here than Silas is.

Once they've absorbed what's going on, the men at the pub treat Silas kindly. Eliot moves inside his mind to describe the effect of this. A vague sensation of blurry faces, voices, and the fire's warmth unlocks Silas' heart, and a new kind of feeling starts to grow inside him (note the plant imagery). The news transforms Silas' reputation: The superstitious villagers imagine that the Devil robbed Silas, so he must not be one of the Devil's helpers. Everyone chimes in with his own opinion. Mr. Snell, the peacemaker, tries to convince Silas of Jem's innocence. And Mr. Macey, who believes in authority, starts talking about the proper legal proceedings.

NOTE: Memory Mr. Macey's remark about accusing the innocent arouses Silas' memory of his own false accusation years ago. The force of memory is important for George Eliot. Remembering his mother's death helped Silas rediscover his herbal medicines to cure Sally Oates in Chapter 2. He tried to forget his past in Lantern-Yard, but remembering it is good for him now, giving him compassion for Jem.

Silas is jolted by Mr. Macey's words into withdrawing his accusation of Jem. This takes a great effort, however—it's excruciating to give up his hope of recovering his money. The men around him don't seem to understand his inarticulate pain. Mr. Macey makes a dry joke about Silas' money being in Hell. Dowlas the farrier suggests that Silas missed the thief's footprints because of his poor eyesight ("eyes . . . like an insect's," he says). Officiously, Dowlas lays out the procedure for inspecting the premises and offers to serve as a deputy. But at least he's willing to get involved. Everyone in the room, in fact, agrees that it's their duty as respectable men to take action. How would the men of your neighborhood act if a local eccentric came running to them wildly for help?

Of course, the men get bogged down in another silly quarrel, over whether the farrier can serve as a deputy. (As a veterinarian, he usually puts on airs of being a doctor, and doctors are traditionally excused from constables' duties.) Imagine Silas sitting there, shivering and waiting for them to resolve this dispute. How would you feel in his place?

CHAPTER 8

The other side of Raveloe—the gentry's world—seems unconnected to the goings-on at the Rainbow. Eliot briefly mentions Godfrey, returning from his party to find that Dunstan hasn't come home. This doesn't seem very important. In the morning, however, Godfrey is swept up in the news about Silas, just as everyone else in town is.

Think about hometown crime cases that are covered on your local television news. They unfold with new evidence daily. This is what happens in Raveloe. A tinder-box is discovered near the stone-pit, and people argue over whether it's a useful piece of evidence. Eliot reports the tides of gossip with irony. Everyone has his or her own theory of the case. Mr. Macey thinks the Devil stole the gold, but when Mr. Tookey says constables shouldn't investigate the Devil's crimes, Macey has to defend the authority of constables. Mr. Snell's theory is that a gypsy peddler he saw a month ago was the thief. The other constables respond to this theory eagerly—aliens like gypsies are logical criminal suspects to them. Somehow, the question of whether the gypsy was wearing earrings becomes crucial. Everybody in town has a different opinion; they all feel it's their duty to solve the mystery. And of course all this discussion takes place at the Rainbow, giving the men an excuse to congregate there.

Silas would like to believe the peddler is the thief, but he's too honest to invent incriminating stories as everybody else has. The villagers, however, ignore Silas' testimony clearing the peddler, preferring their own stories. How do you think Silas regards all this activity?

At this point, Godfrey appears at the Rainbow. Like Silas, he's out of key with the Raveloe mania—he recalls that the peddler wasn't evil at all. Then he rides away from the village. While there's a public uproar over Silas' robbery, Godfrey investigates his own robbery privately.

Chapter 8

Eliot switches from ironic commentary to direct dramatization now, recording Godfrey's restless thoughts as he rides along. When Godfrey meets Dunstan's friend Bryce, Bryce tells him what happened the other day at the hunt. Bryce is surprised to hear that Dunstan hasn't come home, but he doesn't seem concerned. (Compare this to how seriously the Raveloe villagers take Silas' mishap.) Godfrey isn't as cool and controlled as Bryce, though he tries to be. Because you're inside his thoughts, you can feel his sense of impending doom.

NOTE: Luck Bryce tells Godfrey that Dunstan is a "lucky" fellow—meaning, ironically, that Dunsey's unlucky because he killed Wildfire. Yet Godfrey sees Dunstan as lucky, because he walked away unhurt from the accident. He sees himself as the victim of Dunstan's good luck. ("He'll never be hurt—he's made to hurt other people.") Godfrey doesn't feel lucky because he's haunted by his inner fears.

Riding home, Godfrey sorts out his position. He feels he has to tell his father about Dunstan's losing the money. How strong is Godfrey's moral sense? His main reason for confessing is that he's sure he'll be found out. He won't, however, take the blame for squandering the rent money himself. He feels, too, that he should confess everything, including his marriage. But he has practical reasons for this: Molly herself might show up at the Red House soon.

Eliot now gives you Godfrey's view of his father—

and it isn't pleasant. The Squire seems hard, like a rock, yet he's a lazy landlord and a lazy father. Godfrey focuses on aspects of the Squire's personality that he resents and fears, making it harder than ever to make up his mind. Have you ever gone back and forth like this over a question? If so, you'll know that you never stop until you're finally forced into action. Godfrey goes to sleep with good intentions, but he sees things differently the next morning. His old habits of cowardly thought return to sap his resolve. Eliot's spent a lot of time showing you what Godfrey is thinking of doing, or planning to do. But the real test is what a man actually does. What do you think Godfrey will say to his father?

CHAPTER 9

Breakfast rituals at the Red House say a lot about the Cass family. The family doesn't eat together. There is no hunger here—the table is spread with food—the Squire even has to take a morning walk to work up an appetite. When he does sit down, he feeds meat to his dog—enough for a poor man's Sunday dinner—before he bothers to eat anything himself. He drinks ale for breakfast, too, which villagers only do on holidays.

Eliot's description of the Squire is mostly negative, but he does carry himself with dignity. She claims this comes from having gone through life believing he was better than the people around him. Eliot believed that human characters are formed by their environments. Watch how other characters' physical bearing expresses how they've been treated for years.

Chapter 9

The Squire, who may have been based on landowners Eliot's father worked for, is a classic reactionary. He's convinced that the younger generation is worthless and that the world's going to pot. His grumbling makes it hard for Godfrey to start his confession. Finally, Godfrey blurts out his problem about the lost rent money. The Squire flies into a rage, just as Godfrey expected.

Instinctively, the Squire zooms in on the crux of the question—why did Godfrey lend Dunstan the money in the first place? Although Godfrey tries to deflect his father's anger onto Dunstan, the Squire soon turns back onto Godfrey. Godfrey isn't a very good liar, but he isn't honest enough to come out with the whole truth. He says he gave the money to Dunstan because of "young men's fooleries." This triggers the Squire's prejudices and distracts him.

NOTE: Fatherhood The Squire seems to relate to his sons only through their need for money or their hope of inheriting his property. In a rage, he threatens to disinherit them and start a new family. He reminds Godfrey that the property isn't entailed (under British law, entailed property had to be passed down to the owner's eldest male successor). He warns Godfrey that Godfrey would benefit from helping the property be run better. The Squire's an insecure father—he compares himself constantly to what "some fathers" do, and he speaks of how his grandfather ran things. In the end, he blames Godfrey's faults on Godfrey's mother, as if disclaiming all fatherhood. Silas, in contrast to Godfrey, seems to have no father. As you read on, look for other examples of good and bad fathers.

Often, Eliot doesn't describe her characters physically, because she wants to focus on their inner moral workings. This scene is dramatized to focus on Godfrey. You see the Squire's gestures and expressions, but you feel Godfrey's reactions.

What is your opinion of Godfrey here? Some readers point out that he does tell the first half of his story honestly. But his father's reaction is so violent, he loses courage. The more you see of Squire Cass, these readers feel, the more you pity Godfrey. In the midst of this scene, he wishes his father had disciplined him more.

Other readers, however, think Godfrey has no excuse. The Squire hasn't even punished him for losing the money, yet as soon as his father comes close to guessing his deeper secret—his marriage—Godfrey turns coward. These readers say it's easy for Godfrey to blame his father for indulging him, just as it's easy for Squire Cass to blame his dead wife for his son's weakness, but people should accept responsibility for their own mistakes.

Ironically, the Squire mentions Nancy Lammeter, not knowing how closely she relates to Godfrey's other problems. In this dialogue, you learn more about Godfrey's courtship of Nancy—there's been an understanding between them for a while, and Nancy has already turned down a proposal from her cousin. You learn that she's pretty, and her home is probably more refined than the Casses'. Read this scene twice—from the Squire's point of view and then from Godfrey's. In the Squire's eyes, Godfrey isn't acting like a man. But feel the pressure Godfrey is under, from his father and from his own desire for Nancy, while he can only evade the issue.

The Squire ends this discussion abruptly, ordering Godfrey around like a servant. Casually, he disowns Dunstan—for the time being, at least. Godfrey escapes from the room, but is his position improved? He hasn't been punished, but he hasn't cleared his conscience, either. What's more, he has a new fear—that the Squire will speak to Mr. Lammeter about Nancy. He hopes, however, that good fortune will keep him out of trouble. Eliot asks you to look at this impulse as a universal human reflex. In a series of parallel sentences, each structured with the phrases "Let him . . . and he will," she gives everyday examples of this impulse at work. But such a faith in Fortune, she declares, ignores the fact that a natural chain of events follows from every human action—"the orderly sequence by which the seed brings forth a crop after its kind."

CHAPTER 10

Eliot switches to a tone of irony as she returns to the more public Raveloe scene. Mockingly, she describes the vain efforts to find the gypsy peddler. Meanwhile, she says, nobody seems concerned that Dunstan still hasn't come home.

NOTE: The mystery For you, unlike the villagers, the real mystery here is Dunstan's disappearance. You know Dunstan disappeared after robbing Silas. Why hasn't anyone in Raveloe made the connection? To some readers, this is a flaw in the plot. Yet Eliot explains that Godfrey is too blinded by an image of Dunstan off enjoying himself. And the villagers simply can't imagine that a member of the gentry would be involved with sordid theft. Some other readers suggest that Eliot has kept these two Raveloe worlds so far apart that it's easy to forget they ever connect with one another. Do you find this part of the plot believable?

People in town still speculate about Silas' robbery, but interest has died down. Eliot focuses your attention now on Silas, who's been offstage for a while. His loss has made him more shrunken and withered than ever. In retrospect, the author suggests his gold was good because it kept his emotions alive (gold's value changes again). Silas feels cut off from life—yet life is beginning to reach out to him. His loss has changed his reputation in town; now people feel sorry for him. Eliot talks about how clumsy such kindness can be—but it's still well meant.

Her first dramatized example is of Mr. Macey, stopping by the cottage to chat. Listen to his typical thoughtless speech as if you were Silas—which phrases would make you wince? Silas, however, sits there dumbly, too crushed to respond.

The next caller, Dolly Winthrop, is more sensitive. Her role in Raveloe is as a nurse, mourner, and sympathizer. She puts up with her husband Ben's sharp jokes, but her natural inclination is toward sad, serious matters. She's drawn to the cottage by Silas' suffering.

Chapter 10

NOTE: Church-going Both Mr. Macey and Dolly think it's important for Silas to start going to church. Neither one, however, is pushing religion on him. Going to church is important for Raveloers because it is neighborly. It isn't necessary to go every week, Eliot tells you, but it is important to go on holy days, when the sacrament (communion) is given. This forms a bond with others in the community. Notice how important the outward forms of church-going are to both of them. Compare the Raveloe attitude toward church-going to your community's attitude. How are they different? How are they alike?

When Dolly knocks at Silas' door, Eliot describes his reaction to this visit in more detail than she did with Mr. Macey's. A need for other people is faintly stirring in Silas. Dolly offers him her homemade lard-cakes, speaking gently.

Dolly is surprised that Silas can read the letters she traced on the tops of the cakes—I.H.S.—which she copied from the pulpit-cloth at church. Though Dolly doesn't know the formal meaning of these letters (they stand for the Greek spelling of "Jesus"), she has the spirit right. Silas, on the other hand, can read, but these letters weren't part of his church's rituals so he can't understand their spirit. Similarly, he doesn't understand the meaning of church bells, which weren't rung in Lantern-Yard. His sect referred to worship as "chapel," so he doesn't even share the meaning of the word "church" with Dolly. Then Dolly expresses the spirit of her religion—a faith that comforts her through life's troubles. She trusts in God and Heaven, although her concept is almost pagan—she sees a group of divinities, "Them as are above us." This is totally different from the religion Silas knew, and he can't even imagine it.

Silas has a hard time communicating with Dolly because he isn't used to talking with people. Yet he's trying. Dolly has brought her little boy Aaron with her, and Silas quietly offers him some cake. Dolly thinks it's good for Silas to have contact with a child (watch for another child to enter his life soon). But shortsighted Silas can hardly see Aaron's face—he's still withdrawn from humanity. Aaron sings a Christmas carol, but Silas' ears aren't used to music—just as his soul isn't used to kindness—and he can't enjoy it.

Dolly leaves, with a last bit of advice to give up working on a Sunday. (This is partly because it's against church law, and partly because of old superstitions.) Silas is relieved to be left alone. Eliot paints a bleak picture of his lonely Christmas day. Possessed by grief, he still doesn't lock his door; he thinks of his cottage as "his robbed home." Eliot adds a sad, short paragraph contrasting him to his loving, trusting youthful self. He is now at his lowest point.

In comparison, the villagers have a merry Christmas, full of traditional celebrations. In the world of the gentry, though, Squire Cass' party on New Year's Eve is the big event, and Eliot describes the eager preparations for it. (No one worries about Dunstan's absence.) Only Godfrey looks forward to the party with conflicting emotions. Eliot dramatizes this in a dialogue between hopeful Godfrey and his demon Anxiety. He seems literally split in two. Compare Silas and Godfrey at this point. Which do you feel sorrier for? Why?

CHAPTER 11

After hearing so much about her, at last you meet Nancy Lammeter, riding to the Casses' party. Eliot tries not to idealize Nancy. Though she's lovely, she's dressed in dowdy clothes. Clinging to her father's waist, glancing nervously down at the mud, she appears unselfconscious. As you read the rest of this chapter, however, you may see why some readers regard Nancy as too good to be true.

You enter Nancy's thoughts as she approaches the house and sees Godfrey. She's embarrassed and confused by the way he's been acting lately. More than that, she disapproves of his reputation. Her pride tells her she deserves a good man like her father. Nevertheless, when Godfrey lifts her off the horse, her emotions go into a tailspin. Clearly, she cares more for him than she'd like to admit.

NOTE: Social history This scene depicts in detail the customs of the gentry. The great houses were far apart, so guests had to ride long distances over bad roads. Parties therefore lasted a good while, to make it worth the trip. Ladies sent their party dresses ahead and changed out of muddy riding clothes when they arrived. Women's styles of the era were high-waisted dresses with long straight skirts, cut low to reveal the neck and shoulders. Men wore long-tailed dinner jackets and short, tight trousers.

You've heard various characters mention the Kimbles and the Osgoods; now you meet them. The Lammeters are greeted by Mrs. Kimble, the Squire's sister and wife of the Raveloe doctor. Upstairs, Nancy meets her other aunt, dignified Mrs. Osgood. Her son Gilbert is the cousin whom Nancy refused to marry.

Mrs. Osgood has brought to the party the two Miss Gunns. Being from a large provincial town, they think they're superior to country folk. But they're impressed with Nancy's grace, beauty, and extraordinary neatness—an outsider's opinion that confirms what Eliot has already told you. The only flaw they see is her rough hands. Nancy isn't ashamed of her hands, though—work is important to her.

NOTE: Dialect The Raveloe gentry have a country accent. Eliot doesn't write their speeches in dialect because Victorian readers expected major characters to use standard English. This accent, however, distinguishes Nancy from the Miss Gunns. Ironically, they too have an accent—but they think theirs is the right one. (How is this trivial prejudice related to the religious prejudices in the previous chapter?) Although the Miss Gunns dwell on this difference, Eliot remarks that Nancy is more of a lady than they are, despite her lack of education.

Next you see Nancy beside another Raveloe lady, her sister Priscilla. By comparison, Nancy's special qualities shine out. Priscilla definitely talks like a country girl. The same dress that makes Nancy look lovely makes Priscilla look sallow and dumpy. Nancy, however, insists that as sisters they should dress alike. (What does this tell you about Nancy?) Priscilla does have common sense. Compare her realistic attitude toward staying home and keeping house for their father (as George Eliot did) to Nancy's high-minded reluctance about Godfrey.

Downstairs at tea, Nancy reflects that marrying Godfrey would make her mistress of this house. She admits to herself that she loves him but her morals won't let her unbend. Eliot speaks of this as Nancy's "inward drama." Do you think she approves or disapproves of Nancy's attitude?

While Godfrey and Nancy sit silently, highly conscious of each other, the rest of the party comes alive. Squire Cass is in a loud, merry, patronizing mood. Mr. Lammeter sits in self-contained dignity. Dr. Kimble busily chats to everyone in the room. Eliot points out that these people aren't aristocrats. The Squire's comments about Godfrey and Nancy are boorish. Even Dr. Kimble is not a great doctor—he inherited his practice. Imagine how Godfrey and Nancy feel as they sit here.

Music, which is so important to Raveloe, is introduced by white-haired Solomon Macey, the fiddler. He respects the gentry but he respects his music, too, and it gives him a special role. He plays the tunes people expect to hear, old songs rich in memories. Music gives him power over them, like a Pied Piper, as he leads the party into the parlor to dance.

Not only are all the gentry here, selected villagers round out the scene. An elaborate social ritual is at work, which everyone seems to enjoy. The villagers comment as they watch the gentry dance, much as people today may comment upon a TV show they're watching. From this quarter, you get another view of Nancy and Godfrey. The villagers agree on Nancy's beauty, but opinion on Godfrey is divided.

An accident (fate or bad luck?) calls Nancy and Godfrey off the dance floor. Nancy's dress has been torn, and she must sit in the next room until Priscilla can help her fix it. Eliot presents the lovers' conversation dramatically, letting you know just enough of what each is feeling to add an undertone of passion to the careful banter. Godfrey tries to tell Nancy he loves her. She rebuffs him coldly, firmly, but with a trace of hurt pride that gives him hope. Even after Priscilla arrives, Godfrey stays near, hanging on to these few moments with Nancy.

CHAPTER 12

Just then, while Godfrey is happily forgetting his marriage, his wife is headed toward the Red House. This isn't a coincidence—she chose this night deliberately so she could shame Godfrey in public. She wants revenge because he insulted her. His own actions brought on this impending doom.

Eliot's portrait of this woman is brief but complex. One side of Molly knows that her addiction to opium is to blame for her wretched life. Yet the other side resents Godfrey for living better and blames him for her misery. Eliot reminds you that Molly is limited by her uncultured past. Throughout this commentary, however, Eliot also remarks that most of us react the same way Molly does to our own misery.

Chapter 12

Molly, like Godfrey, lacks moral strength. In this scene, her weakness is conveyed in many ways. The falling snow literally makes her slow down and get lost. The snow also symbolizes her moral weakness, which makes it hard for her to get anywhere in life. Her addiction to opium is another weakness. She turns to it when she's in pain and needs comfort. She hesitates, knowing it will hurt her baby, yet she gives in to her selfish craving. The drug, however, makes her even weaker, and the snow soon completely numbs her.

Molly's love for her child is the one thing that fights against her drug addiction. But is she a good mother? Her child is ragged and hungry, a burden that she clutches automatically. She ultimately chooses the opium over her child's welfare, and under the influence of the drug she stops caring about what happens to the baby. On the other hand, there is a tender bond between them. The little girl sleeps peacefully, and when she tumbles awake she cries "mammy" and struggles to climb back into her mother's arms.

The scene shifts to the child's viewpoint. Easily distracted, she sees a bright light and runs after it. She can't see what it is—she seems nearsighted, like Silas Marner.

NOTE: Parallels A few chapters ago, Dunstan Cass was attracted by a bright light shining from Silas' cottage. In this parallel scene, the baby also is drawn by the firelight into Silas' home. Silas was out on a simple errand before. This time, he's left the door open because he has fallen into one of his mysterious fits. Ironically, he was looking out the door, hoping his gold would come back to him, just as the golden-haired child is heading toward the cottage.

The little girl toddles straight into Silas' cottage and falls asleep by the fire. Eliot now backtracks slightly to show why Silas' door was open. Pathetically, he believed the villagers' superstition about his gold returning to him on New Year's Eve, and he was looking for his treasure. Why does he have a fit just then? Some readers think it's chance; others think it's a sign of a mystical power running his life.

When Silas comes out of his fit, he turns toward the fireplace. Two logs have fallen apart and he pushes them together. (What could this symbolize?) His nearsighted eyes notice a gleam of gold on the hearth. He thinks at first that it's his money, and his heart pounds. Then the gold starts to move, to come alive (he used to imagine his gold was alive). He touches it. It is not cold and hard, but soft and warm.

When Silas' gold disappeared, he tried to find a logical explanation. Now, however, he's ready to accept a magical explanation for the appearance of the child. He wonders if she is his little sister, come to him in a dream. This memory stirs long-dead emotions in him, and symbolically he also stirs the fire brighter. More memories rush into his mind. Remnants of his old religious feelings revive, and he senses "some Power presiding over his life." This child may be something new in his life, but his feelings for her grow out of his past.

When the little girl wakes, Silas is forced into

action. He picks her up and instinctively hushes her cries. (Notice that she still cries "mammy"—it's a natural reflex.) Taking care of her occupies his mind totally, the way weaving and counting his gold did. Although he's slow and a little shy, he figures out how to fulfill her needs. He feeds her, generously giving her sugar he wouldn't have used for himself. He awkwardly wrestles off her tiny, wet shoes. Finally, however, he realizes that she must have come in from outside. He tracks her footprints out into the cold night until he finds her mother, lying covered in snow.

CHAPTER 13

Back at the Red House, the party is in full swing. Eliot takes a few paragraphs to flesh out the scene, describing the rooms as precisely as a stage set, slipping into various characters' minds. She is inside Godfrey's thoughts when an unexpected visitor appears at the door. Through Godfrey's eyes, your attention is focused not on Silas but on the child in his arms. Godfrey immediately recognizes his own child.

NOTE: Parallels Silas interrupts this scene just as he did the scene at the Rainbow in Chapter 7. In both scenes he appears like a ghost. Here, however, rather than a literal specter, he's a ghostly reminder of Godfrey's double life.

Eliot shows you this scene on two levels: the outer public event and Godfrey's inner reaction to it. The men in charge respond discreetly to Silas' news about the woman he's found in the snow, keeping the shocking news from the ladies. The ladies, however, press around Silas, naturally attracted to the pretty baby. Meanwhile Godfrey's thoughts are in turmoil, though he fights to look calm. Unlike Dunstan, who'd probably regard this as good luck, Godfrey is afraid his wife isn't really dead—and he's ashamed of that feeling.

Silas makes a startling announcement—that he plans to keep the child. He speaks of this as his "right," as though she were a prize he'd won. She does cling to him, trusting him more than the motherly women around her. No one seems to take Silas' announcement seriously, however.

Like the men at the Rainbow, these people stir themselves to help Silas. There are limits, however, to their charity. Mrs. Kimble is reluctant to touch the dirty baby. The Squire suggests to Kimble to send his apprentice to the woman in the snow instead of going himself. To the public eye, Godfrey appears to be helping out of a sense of duty. What do you think his real motives are? Notice how his daughter's cry tears at his heart, as if a plant ("some fibre") were growing there. Eliot emphasizes his emotional state with one detail—the thin dress shoes that, in his hurry, he wears out into the snow. Dolly Winthrop, whom he fetches for help, ironically praises him for going to such trouble. Later, his uncle Kimble tells him it was silly for him to come out to help. It seems the gentry aren't expected to help the way villagers are.

As Godfrey wrestles with his conscience, waiting to hear if his wife is dead, he feels responsible for his child. He considers acknowledging her, which he knows is the right thing to do. But he realizes that if he doesn't, he'll be able to marry Nancy. Love for Nancy, not just shame over his wife, pushes him toward moral cowardice. In Silas' cottage, he takes one last look at his wife, who's been pronounced dead. (Eliot calls her "unhappy," which can mean unlucky as well as miserable.) What do you think Godfrey feels as he looks at her?

NOTE: Foreshadowing Eliot tells you that, sixteen years later, Godfrey will tell the "full story of this night." Thus, you know Godfrey won't tell his secret now, but in the future something will make him tell all. This sixteen year period will complete the symmetry of the plot (it's been sixteen years since Silas' loss of faith). At this moment, Godfrey is at the peak of his fortune, while Silas has just passed the bottom of his. Another sixteen years may change their positions.

Godfrey turns to see Silas cradling the child in his arms. Eliot describes the baby's peaceful presence as a sacred, natural thing, and Godfrey is affected by it. How do you think he feels when she turns her eyes away to gaze lovingly at Silas? Remember this scene—it will be re-enacted later.

Godfrey nonchalantly discusses the child's fate with the "withered" weaver. Silas stubbornly repeats his intention to keep her. You don't enter his feelings but you hear his reasons. The first one is logical enough—he senses a kinship with her, as two lonely, abandoned creatures. The second reason is more irrational—he thinks she's come to replace his gold. Silas' mind isn't working clearly, but his heart is. In contrast, Godfrey's heart seems confused while his mind is working busily. He doesn't protest; he hands Silas some money and leaves quickly. His conversation with Dr. Kimble as they head home reflects public opinion—Silas should keep the baby because no one else will.

As Godfrey returns to the party, his anxiety ebbs away. Knowing his secret is safe, he feels relieved and carefree. Except for the nagging possibility that Dunstan may come home and spill the truth, he faces his future optimistically. He tells himself he's doing the best thing for his child. Read carefully how Eliot describes his reasoning. Do you think she sympathizes with him or condemns him? Does this psychological portrait seem realistic—like the way people you know would think and behave?

CHAPTER 14

Although Molly's death is hardly noticed by the world at large, Eliot says, it seems to have a purpose, setting off a chain of events that will affect many people. One of the first changes is in Silas. His decision to keep the child makes the villagers more sympathetic to him than ever. As before, Dolly Winthrop personifies the best of Raveloe behavior, bringing a pile of baby clothes and helping give the baby a bath. Silas' and Dolly's religions seem more in tune with each other now. Dolly believes

Chapter 14

heavenly spirits brought the child to Silas. Silas believes the child came from an unknown place, the same one where his gold disappeared—he links the two events in a pattern. Dolly agrees, with her almost pagan belief in the rhythms of nature and the great mysterious workings of fate.

Dolly offers to help care for the baby. Silas, still a miser, is determined to do everything, to keep the baby's love for himself. But he is willing to let Dolly, an experienced mother, teach him the "mysteries" of child care. ("Mystery" here means "sacred rites" as well as "unknown questions.") One piece of advice she gives him troubles him, though. She insists he bring the child into the church. Dolly believes in christening the same way she believes in giving children their shots ("noculation")—to protect them from every possible harm. Silas is baffled because he doesn't know the word "christening" (in Lantern-Yard it was called "baptism"). As he speaks of his own religion in a low voice, he still seems bitter. But he agrees to do whatever is good for the child. As he thus moves beyond his own interests, his memory is reawakened. He decides to name the baby Hepzibah, after his mother and sister—though Dolly suggests he shorten it to Eppie. She wishes Silas good luck—which she says comes to anyone who does the right deeds.

Since no one knows whether Eppie's been baptized, the rector has to decide which is riskier—possibly baptizing her twice, or possibly not baptizing her at all. (Remember Mr. Macey's concern over the Lammeter's wedding ceremony?) He decides to baptize her, and Silas goes to church for the ceremony. With the spirit of faith dead inside him, he can't interpret what's going on, but he goes for Eppie's sake.

NOTE: Gold Eliot compares Eppie to the gold that she has replaced in Silas' life. The gold is hidden and cold, but Eppie is associated with nature, sunlight, growing things, and bird songs. While the gold carried his thoughts inward, Eppie forces them outward. While the gold isolated him, Eppie demands ties to other people. The gold made him blind and deaf, but Eppie awakens his senses. To carry this beyond metaphor, Eliot shows Silas and Eppie actually going out into the sunshiny day, picking flowers in a meadow, listening to birds.

Eliot suggests that Silas is like an insect—an old fly, sluggish after a long winter, who now basks in the spring sunshine. Out in the meadow with Eppie, Silas rediscovers an important part of his past—herbs. Eliot points out that Silas' regeneration is not so much a matter of learning new things as coming to terms with the past and opening up his feelings, like a blooming flower.

Dolly warns Silas that children must be disciplined. She recommends either spanking or shutting them up in the coal-closet (as she does with Aaron). Silas hates the idea of punishing Eppie. One day, however, while he's busy weaving, she gets hold of his scissors and cuts the strip of cloth that ties her to the loom so she can't run away. She runs outside, attracted as usual by the bright light. When Silas can't find her, he's as terrified as he was when he lost his gold. He searches around the stone-pit frantically, imagining the worst. Then he searches the meadow and the neighboring field, straining his weak eyes. Finally he finds her beside a shallow pond, playing happily in the mud, oblivious to the panic he's just gone through. Like most parents in such situations, Silas is so relieved that at first all he does is kiss her and hold her tight. Back at the cottage, however, he decides to take Dolly's advice and see if punishment will improve Eppie's behavior. He scolds her and unwillingly puts her into the little closet by the hearth for a minute. Then he spends half an hour cleaning her—only for her to climb happily back into the hole as soon as his back is turned. As he later tells Dolly, this is his last try at discipline—he'll just hope Eppie outgrows her mischievous stage. What does this scene tell you about Eppie? What does it tell you about Silas?

Once again you see the public view of Silas changing. As he takes Eppie with him on his business calls, customers greet him as a real person. His obvious love for the child makes him less frightening to others.

Eppie gives him a purpose in life, too. For her, he must be in touch with the community. He appreciates money again because he can use it for her. Notice Eliot's imagery; she compares Eppie to a young plant, and Silas to the gardener who helps it grow. The chapter's final paragraph celebrates the power a child can have to save men's souls. Eliot says these children fulfill a role angels used to play. What does that tell you about Eliot's religious beliefs?

CHAPTER 15

While Silas is opening up through his love for Eppie, in contrast you see Godfrey's narrow, hidden love for his child. He watches her with an interest that he can't show publicly. He gives Silas money from time to time, but he doesn't dare do it too often.

Eliot says Godfrey isn't too worried about Eppie growing up in a humble cottage. You'll have to decide for yourself whether it's Godfrey or George Eliot who believes that "people in humble stations often were . . . happier . . . than those who are brought up in luxury." In the next paragraph, however, it is clearly Eliot speaking. She refers to an old fairy tale, where a magic ring pricked its owner when he followed his own desires instead of duty. She suggests that this pinprick was not painful at first—only later. You've just seen Godfrey choose his desire for Nancy over his duty to Eppie. What does this fairy-tale image suggest about Godfrey's future?

The public view of Godfrey is positive—bright-eyed and firm. Now that Dunstan seems gone for good, Godfrey finds it easy to follow a straight path, because it leads straight to marrying Nancy. Inside, though, Godfrey is different from what the world sees (just as Silas was different from his local legend during his long exile). Godfrey is conscious of having been "delivered from temptation"—curiously using religious language, instead of the language of luck, for the first time.

As Godfrey looks hopefully toward his future with Nancy, one of the most important elements of his domestic visions is their children. This leads him naturally to think of his other child. He doesn't envision her clearly—she seems just a sexless "it." But he calms his conscience by promising himself to provide money for her—that's his duty. Eliot stresses this comment with a touch of irony. What should a "father's duty" be, according to Eliot?

PART TWO
CHAPTER 16

This chapter opens in autumn, a time for reaping harvests. Most of Part One was set in winter—a cold, dead season that suited Silas' exile. In contrast, Silas' first years with Eppie were described as springtime—when new life grows.

NOTE: In Shakespeare's play *The Winter's Tale*, sixteen years elapse between Act III and Act IV. The mood changes from winter to spring. During the elapsed time, King Leontes has changed. His teenage daughter, Perdita, who's associated with flowers and nature, is finally restored to him in Act V. Eliot, as an ardent Shakespeare reader, probably intended a similar change between the "acts" in *Silas Marner*.

In sixteen years, Raveloe hasn't changed much—the church bells ring cheerfully after Sunday services, and the congregation files out in order of social rank. But individuals have changed. Godfrey is a handsome, middle-aged man. His wife Nancy has lost her youthful glow, but in its place there is a mature beauty. Eliot hints that Nancy's experience has sobered her. What do you imagine her experience has been?

Silas, who now looks old, makes a picturesque contrast next to Eppie, the embodiment of youth and high spirits. Her curly auburn hair suggests an inner nature that isn't docile. Nevertheless, Eliot shows you, Eppie has neat, tidy habits—a virtue Eliot praised before in Nancy. Eppie has a good-looking admirer, at first introduced merely as a village lad. The fact that she has an admirer underscores her beauty and signals that a shift in generations has taken place. Soon, however, as the young man joins them, you learn that he is Aaron Winthrop. In the conversation that follows, Eliot establishes the characters' lives. Silas still works hard and dotes on Eppie. Aaron earns his living as a skilled gardener. Dolly and Aaron are as close as family to Silas and Eppie. Godfrey has given Silas and Eppie a lot of financial help, which they accept innocently, with respect.

NOTE: Gardens Eppie's wish for a garden fits in with a cluster of plant imagery here. Eppie, a child of nature, has a mystical relation to flowers—she thinks they can hear people. Nourishing souls, like Dolly, are identified with gardens. Aaron's talent for gardening gives him great value in the eyes of the gentry, who cannot grow their own gardens. Flowers also signify domestic happiness. Aaron is going to plant lavender for Eppie, which traditionally was planted by a man for his new bride. (Notice that there's a big bed of lavender at the Red House. What could this symbolize?) Silas, however, is only interested in the garden for Eppie's sake. Later, he suggests that they build a fence to protect their garden. What could this symbolize? Do you think it's a positive or a negative impulse?

Eppie's attachment to nature is shown also in the animals around her. On the way home, she scratches a friendly donkey's nose. (Some readers think this donkey represents Silas. What do you think of that interpretation?) A lively little dog and a litter of cats also live in their cottage. The cottage has changed; it's now cozy and clean. But the hearth hasn't been altered, because Silas is attached to it as part of his past. Eppie cooks Silas' Sunday dinner and fusses over him, making him go smoke his pipe while she tidies up.

Eliot reports the Raveloe opinion of this situation. Godfrey is admired for his charity to Silas (you know, however, what Godfrey's real motives are). Silas is admired for raising Eppie. Mr. Macey even says, superstitiously, that Silas' money will come back to him as a reward for this. As Silas smokes, however, you learn that he hasn't been totally transformed. He adopts village customs only for Eppie's sake. He's been able to get a perspective on his past, however, by talking with Dolly about his false accusation in Lantern-Yard. Eliot reports this conversation in a flashback, so you can watch Silas reconciling himself to his past. Note that contact with another human being, Dolly, helps him to gain perspective.

Notice how Silas reverts to biblical language— "clave to me," "lifted up his heel again' me"—to describe his trial. His story confuses Dolly, because Lantern-Yard's rituals are so different from hers. But her faith in God's goodness sustains her, and she advises Silas that he should have trusted God.

Dolly uses common sense and human feeling to find a reason for Silas' accusation. Inarticulate Dolly can't sort it out immediately—she needs to think about it while she's actively engaged with life. One night, while mourning a dead neighbor, she's inspired. She accepts her inability to understand every event. She's seen plenty of sorrow, and she can't see the reason for it, but she feels certain—"I feel it i' my own inside"— that it has a larger purpose. She tells Silas that he shouldn't have abandoned his community— that, to her mind, is the big sin, not turning his face against God. Dolly doesn't insist dogmatically on her solution, though, when Silas points out that it's hard to forgive people sometimes. He does agree with her, however, that there's some large, mysterious good working in the world— that's why Eppie was sent to him. "There's dealings with us," he sums it up.

Silas has told Eppie the story of his finding her. She knows everything he knows about her mother, but she's never been curious about her father. Eliot attributes this to Eppie's purity of mind, a result of her secluded upbringing. (Some readers think Eliot makes Eppie too perfect here. Compare this to Eliot's portrayal of Nancy in Chapter 11.) But, trying to paint a realistic portrait of country life, Eliot points out that not all country children are this innocent. Eppie is also different from other village girls because she's slight and delicate. Do you think Eppie's set apart because of her birth or because of her upbringing?

Like Silas, Eppie is attached to old things—the furze bush her mother was found under, and the old stone-pit. Silas tells her that the water in the pit is going down because Godfrey Cass is draining some fields. This sign of change leads them to talk of another change: Aaron has asked Eppie to marry him. Silas seems anxious—what do you think is going through his mind? Eppie sees this marriage as a way to make Silas' old age easier, for Aaron would come to live with them. Though she likes Aaron, she doesn't seem to be in love with him. Silas thinks she's too young to be thinking of marriage. Yet he is eager to see Eppie's future settled, and he's learned to be philosophical about change, so he decides to ask Dolly for her advice. How do you feel about this marriage? Do you think that's how Eliot wants you to feel?

CHAPTER 17

As the story moves back to Godfrey's world, you see that the Red House has changed, too. The parlor is still dark, but now it's clean and neat. Like Silas, Nancy has preserved the past—the dead Squire's belongings—but no one touches them. In contrast to the big party you last saw here, it seems empty with only four people here today. Yet there were only two people in the scene before—what does Eliot feel is missing here?

The interchange between Mr. Lammeter and Priscilla shows the shift in generations—Priscilla now manages the farm, and Mr. Lammeter has lost his firm control. Priscilla refuses to stay to tea, saying she needs to get home to watch over the dairymaid. Priscilla blames the girl's approaching marriage for her incompetence. Notice her outburst, a few paragraphs later, about men. Why is she so sour?

As Priscilla and Nancy go for a walk, Eliot uses their conversation to help you catch up on their lives. Priscilla, who enjoys her own work, says running a dairy would keep Nancy's mind off her worries. But Nancy says that a dairy wouldn't lift Godfrey's spirits. After praising her husband, Nancy claims she understands why he frets about not having children. This, then, is their marital problem.

After the Lammeters leave, Godfrey goes to look at the draining fields. Nancy sits alone with her Bible. Unlike Dolly, she can read the Bible. But like Dolly, she isn't a scholar, and the words on the page soon fade away as she meditates on her own life. Anxiously, she muses on her childlessness. She knows Godfrey feels deprived. She wanted children, too, but she can deal with her own sense of loss. She humbly accepted the death of their one baby, fourteen years ago. Since then, she's devoted herself to Godfrey to make up for it. But there's one thing she won't do—adopt a child. Eliot points out that adoption wasn't very common then (as it became in her own time and in ours).

NOTE: Nancy tends to form rigid opinions and cling to them. These are essential to her personality—they grow in her mind like grass, Eliot says (more plant imagery). Nancy formed her code early in life, and formed it out of superstition as well as rational thought. How does Eliot seem to feel about Nancy's principles?

Nancy is convinced that adopting a child would be going against the will of God. You can hear her recalling Godfrey's arguments against this. Interestingly, he talks about adopting a specific child—Eppie. Nancy is talking about a principle, however, and she won't budge. She says it was all right for Silas to adopt Eppie because the child came to him unsought—like Dolly, she accepts the mysterious workings of God. But this doesn't bring her peace.

Eliot digresses to describe Godfrey's own feelings about adopting Eppie. Since you have seen Silas and Eppie together, you can imagine the effect of this adoption on Silas, but Eliot says Godfrey never worries about this. Why not? He believes that anyone would want Eppie to rise in social class. Some readers think Eliot condemns Godfrey for this attitude, for he's really fulfilling his own desire for his child. Others say he can't help his class prejudices, and they point out that Eliot says that he's no longer as bad as he was in Part One.

Back in Nancy's mind, you see she's grateful that Godfrey has been so good to her, in spite of her refusal to adopt a child. Then you go back into Godfrey's mind. He appreciates Nancy's loving attention and understands how important her convictions are to her. But his sense of her firm morals only makes it harder to explain the truth about Eppie. He does love Nancy. But because their marriage is childless, he blames this for his unhappiness. Eliot says this is a common human mistake—life is never entirely happy for anybody, but most people can't accept this. Godfrey aggravates this natural tendency by thinking that he's been denied a child to punish him for his past. Who does he seem to think is punishing him?

Nancy rouses herself from her thoughts with a sense, like Dolly's, that she must just live one day at a time. A servant brings in tea and tells her that people have been running up the road away from the village. Nancy looks out the window. You see that it's a beautiful scene, but in her anxiety it looks ominous to her.

CHAPTER 18

The next chapter is swift and dramatic, as a sudden turn of events draws the story to its climax. Godfrey walks into the room, pale and trembling, and Nancy's relief turns to apprehension. Although he's upset, Godfrey tries to break his news kindly—that Dunstan's skeleton has been found.

NOTE: Dunstan's body has decayed, but he was identified by the objects found with his bones. Godfrey's gold-handled whip lay there, re-creating an image of Dunsey swaggering along the hedgerows. In a way, this represents a part of Godfrey that died along with Dunstan. But along with the whip, other gold objects also survived—Silas' coins. These represent a part of Silas that died.

Although this discovery must have an effect on

Silas, too, Eliot keeps your attention focused only on Nancy and Godfrey. She enters into both of their thoughts, to show you their differing reactions. Godfrey is in shock, remembering the full implications of Dunstan's death. Nancy, however, is fairly calm, thinking of Dunstan only as the family black sheep. When she learns that Dunstan was a thief, she feels a proper sense of family shame, which she imagines Godfrey feels, too.

But something more is bothering him. This incident has convinced him that all secrets come to light eventually, and he's decided to clear his conscience at last. Notice his steady gaze as he looks at her, and his firm language. He talks explicitly about God, rather than the vague fortune he trusted to years ago. Yet he conceives of God as "God Almighty"—a stern, powerful judge, much different from Dolly's benevolent, mysterious image of God. What's your opinion of Godfrey now?

For a moment their eyes meet directly. Godfrey tells his secret, in plain, direct language. Nancy's reaction is hard to gauge—she turns pale but sits quietly. Godfrey seems scared of her, and he goes on talking, trying to justify what he did. The suspense builds as Nancy remains silent.

But when she speaks, her reaction is surprising. She doesn't condemn Godfrey for his former marriage or for hiding the secret. Instead she focuses on the present. Now that she knows that Eppie is Godfrey's child, she wants to adopt her. She only regrets that Godfrey kept this secret so long, depriving them of the child for many years. She knows attachments build over time, and lost time can't be recovered.

Godfrey is amazed that he didn't predict Nancy's reaction better. Have you ever had a moment like this—when someone you thought you knew inside and out revealed new depths? If so, you know how unsettling it is. Godfrey probes Nancy's feelings, testing whether she really disapproves of him or not. But Nancy, like Dolly, believes that the pattern of events is mysterious and that people can't judge the ultimate outcome of their actions. She doesn't completely forgive Godfrey, but she accepts what's done as done. They agree upon their duty now—to go to Marner's cottage and offer to adopt Eppie.

CHAPTER 19

Eliot prevented you from thinking too much about Silas in the previous chapter. But she moves her scene now to Silas' cottage, where Silas sits contentedly with Eppie. His face is transformed by excitement, because his stolen money has been recovered. Now he has both his treasures. But he explains to Eppie that she has become more precious to him than his gold ever was. He would rather not have the gold back, if it meant losing Eppie. He speaks as though some conscious power took the money away, sent Eppie to him, and then returned the money for him and Eppie to use. Ironically, just as he's saying how forsaken he'd feel if he ever lost her, a knock comes at the door. Eppie opens it to see Mr. and Mrs. Cass, as she politely calls them. She doesn't yet know what you know—that they've come to take her from Silas.

In this scene, Eliot lets you know each character's feelings and reactions at each point. In fact, she scarcely describes the physical scene at all,

Chapter 19

concentrating instead on the inner drama. The speeches themselves are dramatic, but Eliot adds to this by letting you feel the emotional currents that run beneath them.

Godfrey begins by referring to that day's discovery. It sounds as if he wants to make things up to Silas for Dunstan's robbery. Godfrey's decided to hide the fact of Eppie's birth, if possible. Subtly, he's working his way toward offering to adopt Eppie as a favor to Silas. Meanwhile, the weaver answers him honestly, showing his usual respect for the upper class. Silas doesn't catch the implications of Godfrey's words at all. He simply says that he and Eppie need no help.

Eppie innocently pipes up that she would like a garden. Nancy immediately responds to this. You've seen before that Eppie is as tidy as Nancy, and that both have strong family feelings. You've also seen that Eppie is unusually well bred for a village girl. Some readers think Eliot is suggesting that Nancy would be a good second mother for Eppie. If so, this adds tension to the dramatic choice Eppie will soon have to make.

This conversation is more difficult for Godfrey than he expected, but he presses on. (Compare the way he acts here to his confrontation with his father in Chapter 9. How has he changed?) He talks vaguely about how Eppie ought to be well taken care of—"she doesn't look like a strapping girl come of working parents," he hints. At this point, Silas seems aware of what Godfrey's driving at, but Eppie still has no idea. Godfrey finally states it clearly: he and his wife want to adopt Eppie. Eliot says Godfrey is tactless—what words in his speech do you think she's referring to?

Eppie instinctively cradles Silas' head in her arm. Remember in Chapter 13 when baby Eppie turned away from Godfrey to touch Silas' face? This is a replay of that scene. Again, Eppie doesn't recognize her biological father. She doesn't feel affected by Godfrey's offer, but she's concerned about Silas, "her father," as she feels him trembling. What do you think Silas is feeling here? Like Nancy in the previous chapter, he answers Godfrey in a surprising way. Unselfishly, he tells Eppie that she may make her own choice. Her choice is a humble, simple, polite "No." She says she feels too attached to her "father" and her familiar social circle.

Godfrey likes to get his own way, and he's annoyed at being turned down. Underneath his noble, beneficent air lie selfish motives. Caught off guard, he blurts out the truth about his relation to Eppie—his "claim" on her. (Remember Silas in Chapter 13 talking about his "right" to Eppie?) Eppie reacts with shock. Silas, however, bolstered by Eppie's refusal, now acts like a protective parent. He chastises Godfrey for abandoning Eppie (and, to his credit, Godfrey feels guilty). Silas rushes on, talking about how sixteen years of daily life together has created feelings between him and Eppie that can't be changed. This gives him a real "right" to Eppie. But Godfrey has never known that kind of intimacy, and he can't understand what Silas is talking about. Patronizingly, he scolds Silas for standing in Eppie's way.

Eppie, listening, is repelled by Godfrey's sanctimonious attitude. Silas, however, takes it to heart and, struggling against his own desires, gives Eppie her choice again. Even Nancy at this point feels sorry for Silas. But she agrees with Godfrey—her code sets blood and class above feeling. Godfrey speaks gently to Eppie, and Nancy echoes his hopeful plea. What do you feel for Godfrey at this moment? for Nancy?

Eppie, however, drops her polite manner. They've passed beyond class roles and face each other as human beings. Clutching Silas' hand, she refuses again in colder tones. She says she simply can't stand to desert Silas, knowing how much he loves her. Silas questions her, making sure she won't regret losing a rich social position. Then Nancy questions her, reminding her of her family duty. But Eppie firmly replies to both that she couldn't live any other life but what she's been brought up to.

Godfrey, agitated, leaves. Nancy tries to cover for his rudeness, then hurries after him.

CHAPTER 20

At the beginning of the previous chapter, maybe you felt sorry for Silas. At the beginning of this one, however, you might just as easily feel sorry for Godfrey and Nancy. Godfrey has been rebuffed by his only child. Nancy has no hope now of ending her childlessness. The silence between them as they arrive home seems brooding, ominous. But then they exchange a long, steady gaze that expresses more than words could ever do. What does this tell you about their marriage?

Godfrey takes Nancy's hand and faces the truth decisively. Notice the imagery he uses. He rejects his own father's images, where human relations are like property—"There's debts we can't pay like money debts." Instead, he uses images of nature to talk of affection—"the trees have been growing."

NOTE: Tragic climax In a letter about *Silas Marner*, Eliot remarked that "the nemesis is mild." Nemesis in Greek tragedy is the hero's punishment for his tragic mistake. Often this is severe—in *Oedipus*, for example, the hero is blinded and exiled. Godfrey's punishment is not severe, but, as he describes it, it's ironic: "I wanted to pass for childless once . . . I shall pass for childless now against my wish."

Godfrey doesn't turn his back on Eppie. Considerately, he decides not to make her parentage public, because it wouldn't do anyone any good. Nevertheless, he intends to go on helping her, playing the role he's always played in her life. Nancy urges him not to tell anyone, even her father and sister, about his secret. Some readers think she's being practical here; others think she's trying to save her own reputation. Godfrey, however, says he'll put the truth in his will—he's given up hiding his secrets.

Like any old married couple, Godfrey and Nancy rehash between them the recent events. Godfrey remarks that Eppie dislikes him, but he accepts this as his fitting punishment. What's more important, he realizes that he still has Nancy—and that's enough. He seems purified of his restless, regretful feelings, ready to be content with his wife and home as they are. All in all, do you think this is a tragic ending to this plot? Why?

CHAPTER 21

Now that the climax of the story has been passed, Eliot resolves the one cloud still hanging over Silas—his early experience in Lantern-Yard. Silas decides to take Eppie to visit his old home. Buoyed by his new perspective on life, he's ready to face the past. Eppie's hopes are simpler—like most country people, she doesn't travel much, and this is an adventure.

When Silas and Eppie arrive in the town, however, it's an alien place. You see it through two perspectives, Silas' inner reaction and Eppie's remarks. Time has caused a change here as it does everywhere, and Silas can't recognize the place. Eppie's confused by the noise and crowds. Even Silas has to ask directions. But he's aware that people won't know where Lantern-Yard is. In Raveloe, everyone knows every house, but in the town a back street is familiar only to the people who live there. Silas seems happy when he recognizes Prison Street and the jail. Eppie, however, is disgusted by this "dark ugly place," which "hides the sky" (as usual, Eppie longs for something natural). The grim jail is a fitting symbol for Silas' old life, yet he's attached to it anyway because it's part of his past.

Have you ever revisited a place you once knew well and found it changed? If so, you may understand Silas' eagerness and puzzlement. The shops on Prison Street have all changed, but he discovers a few familiar landmarks to lead him to Lantern-Yard. When he turns the last corner, though, a rude shock awaits him. The entire street has been knocked down and replaced with a factory.

NOTE: Social history This novel is set in an era of transition, when villages like Raveloe still existed but big industrial cities had already sprung up. This brief picture of urban life intensifies by contrast the picture Eliot has drawn of Raveloe. She presents this manufacturing town and its miserable living conditions with a minimum of description, relying mostly upon her characters' remarks to show it to you. Eppie exclaims at how crowded it is. Even Silas is surprised by the smell. Eliot gives you a quick, unsettling glimpse of dirty faces in dark doorways. The factory produces a dehumanized, faceless stream of men and women.

With her reverence for the past, Eliot stresses how transient this city is. Silas can't find anyone who's lived there longer than ten years. People and places he used to know seem to be swept away, as though they never existed. Compare this to Raveloe, which is rooted in its past. Would you call your own community transient or rooted in the past? What about America in general?

Eliot cuts immediately back to Raveloe, where Dolly helps Silas sort out what happened. Dolly muses that there are many things in life which remain "dark" to ordinary people. Silas agrees, but he says that since Eppie has come to him, "I've had light enough to trusten by"—the darkness of life no longer troubles him.

CONCLUSION

In Chapter 6, Mr. Macey said that winter was a strange season for the Lammeters' wedding. The Lammeters were outsiders, but Eppie isn't—she gets married in spring, the right season. Symbolically, the spring is lovely and fertile, filled with flowers and new life. But Eliot also tells you the villagers' practical reasons why spring is best—they have more time for weddings then, and it's better weather for a light dress.

This wedding scene works to restore a sense of harmony after the crisis in Chapter 19. Eppie accepts her wedding dress from Nancy, smoothing over hard feelings. Godfrey has provided the wedding feast, and soon you'll see he's made additions to Silas' cottage in preparation for Aaron's moving in. Everyone in town, from Priscilla Lammeter to Mr. Macey, is on hand to watch the wedding party walk to church. But there is an undertone of sadness. Nancy needs to be kept company; Godfrey has some vague excuse for being away. How do you think they feel today?

All of the village rituals are observed. Mr. Macey makes a little speech to Silas, blessing the marriage. Guests gather in the churchyard early so they can tell their old stories about Silas and Eppie over again. The men head for the Rainbow after the service.

NOTE: A family Ben Winthrop conveniently goes to the Rainbow so that the final group consists of

Dolly, Aaron, Eppie, and Silas. Sharp-tongued Ben might disrupt this group, which is like a little family. Silas and Dolly have a close partnership; Dolly is like a mother to Eppie. Eppie and Aaron have such an innocent relationship, it seems to some readers to be more like a brother-sister love than a sexual love.

Eliot's own childhood was not totally happy. Her mother seems to have ignored her, and although she was very close to her older brother at first, they fell out with each other later. To some readers, this perfect family picture at the end of this book—"four united people"—is Eliot's nostalgic dream of a family bound by love and respect, not just by blood.

As the wedding party heads home, notice that Eppie's garden is flourishing. Though it's protected, it isn't blocked off from society; an open fence on one side allows flowers to peek through. The novel ends with Eppie's loving, contented comment, "O father, what a pretty home ours is! I think nobody could be happier than we are."

A STEP BEYOND

Tests and Answers
TESTS

Test 1

1. The incriminating clue in the Lantern-Yard robbery is _____
   A. a tinder-box
   B. Silas Marner's pocket-knife
   C. a gold-handled riding whip

2. Silas Marner learned herbal medicine from _____
   A. his mother
   B. a gypsy peddler
   C. the cobbler's wife Sally Oates

3. Godfrey Cass can't marry Nancy Lammeter because _____
   A. his father disapproves of her
   B. she is engaged to her cousin Gilbert Osgood
   C. he is already married

4. Dunstan Cass is attracted to Silas' cottage by _____
   A. the warm fire
   B. the smell of roast pork
   C. the need for money

5. The moderator of events at the Rainbow is _____
   A. Mr. Macey, the old parish-clerk
   B. Ben Winthrop, the wheelwright
   C. Mr. Snell, the landlord

6. When Silas enters the Rainbow, he looks like _____

A. the Devil   B. a ghost
C. a mechanical man

7. Dolly Winthrop's lard-cakes are decorated with _____
   A. a sacred symbol copied from church
   B. the Cass family crest
   C. her initials

8. On New Year's Eve, Silas looks out the door because _____
   A. he's hunting for the thief's footsteps
   B. he thinks his gold might return
   C. he hears a child's cry

9. Raveloers value _____
   I. craftsmanship
   II. neighborliness
   III. social rank
   A. I and II only   B. II and III only
   C. I, II, and III

10. As she grows up, Eppie shows a love for _____
    A. flowers, birds, and animals
    B. fine clothes and polished manners
    C. good deeds and church-going

11. Discuss the parallels between Silas' story and Godfrey's.

12. Which do you think Eliot prefers—Silas' religion or Dolly's? Give evidence from the book.

13. Compare the scene at the Rainbow in Chapter 6 with the scene at the Red House in Chapter 11. What total picture of Raveloe life do they represent?

14. Discuss the importance of family in this novel.

Tests and Answers

15. How does light/dark imagery work in this novel? Relate it to the themes of the book.

Test 2

1. Silas Marner's cottage is located near ____
   A. the church   B. the stone-pit
   C. the highway

2. Silas has fallen into a trance when
   I. the church elder he's nursing in Lantern-Yard dies
   II. Dunstan Cass comes to rob him
   III. Eppie wanders into his cottage
   A. I and II only   B. II and III only
   C. I and III only

3. Dolly Winthrop calls God ____
   A. Our Lord and Master
   B. Them As Are Above
   C. God Almighty

4. The village storyteller is ____
   A. Squire Cass
   B. the old clerk Mr. Macey
   C. young Aaron Winthrop

5. Silas first thinks his gold has been stolen by ____
   A. Jem Rodney, the mole-catcher
   B. a gypsy with earrings
   C. Dunstan Cass

6. When Dunstan Cass doesn't come home, his family ____
   A. starts a manhunt for a mysterious gypsy

B. has the stone-pit drained
C. assumes he has run away

7. Nancy and Priscilla Lammeter dress alike ―――
   because
   A. Nancy thinks sisters should dress the same
   B. Priscilla imitates her sister
   C. Nancy wants to look prettier than Priscilla

8. Molly Farren's weakness is ―――
   A. her desire to be a lady
   B. her love for her baby
   C. her addiction to opium

9. Eppie is attracted to Silas' cottage by ―――
   A. her mother's voice
   B. a bright fire
   C. a playful kitten

10. When Dunstan's skeleton is found, it has ―――
    with it
    A. his brother Godfrey's riding whip
    B. his father's silver tankards
    C. the money he got for selling Wildfire

11. Discuss Silas' cycle of fortune. Is he the victim of circumstance?

12. How does Godfrey change in the course of the novel? Refer to specific scenes.

13. Using various characters, assemble Eliot's picture of the rural gentry. What does her ideal for this class seem to be?

14. What value does the past hold in this novel?

15. Compare Raveloe with the city Silas comes from.

ANSWERS
Test 1
1. B 2. A 3. C 4. A 5. C 6. B
7. A 8. B 9. C 10. A

11. Jot down on scrap paper various elements in Silas' life, and look for parallels in Godfrey's. Then do the reverse—find elements in Godfrey's life that are paralleled in Silas'. These may include: their brothers (Dane and Dunstan), their fiancées (Nancy and Sarah), their relationships to Eppie, or their sixteen-year cycles of exile and redemption.

Begin your answer with a broad statement about the role of parallels in tying the two plots together. Then discuss each element in turn. Show not only the similarities in their stories but also the differences that become apparent when parallel events are contrasted. For example, Silas' fiancée breaks off their engagement when he's falsely accused, but Godfrey becomes engaged to Nancy when his true secret is not revealed. Refer to specific scenes in the book whenever possible. For example, in writing about their differing relationships to Eppie, you might refer to the two scenes when Eppie, first as an infant and then as a grown girl, turns away from Godfrey to touch Silas' face. End with a paragraph looking at the pattern that the parallels create in the novel as a whole, and discussing the symmetry of the novel.

12. Begin by comparing Silas' and Dolly's religions. Dis-

cuss this on several levels: the different words they use, the different rituals they follow, their different concepts of God, and their different religious spirits. Then discuss how these religions affect the plot, referring to specific incidents. For example, Silas' religion creates a tragic situation when he is falsely accused by the drawing of lots. Dolly's religion helps Silas to be incorporated into the community when he takes Eppie to be christened. Finally, define what you think is Eliot's moral scheme in this book. Look at the plot—who gets punished and who is rewarded? Refer also to her own comments. Then show how this moral scheme fits in with either of these two religions.

13. Before you answer, make a list of details, characters, and events for each scene. Find items in the two lists which are similar or in direct contrast. Focus your discussion upon these points. Contrasts might include the fact that the Rainbow group is lower class and all-male, while the Red House group also has upperclass and female characters. Similarities might include the fact that Silas interrupts both scenes, and music and social rituals are important in both. Decide whether there are more contrasts or similarities. Then, in your opening paragraph, make a statement about how similar or different the two scenes are. Following this, you can organize your answer in one of two ways. You can discuss the Rainbow scene first and then the Red House scene. Or you can discuss each point of comparison separately. In your final paragraph, describe the total picture of Raveloe. If you've focused on contrasts, you might say Raveloe is really two different social worlds. If you've focused on similarities, you might say it's a harmonious community, with one set of values for all social classes.

14. Jot down the names of the book's major characters.

Then beside them write names of their family and what the family is like. Don't take the word "family" too literally. It may include adoptive relations, such as Silas and Eppie, or very close friendships, such as Silas and William Dane or Dolly and Eppie. It may even include strong social groups, such as Silas' sect (the "brethren"). You can organize your answer in several different ways, according to whatever pattern you see in this list. For instance, you may want to contrast happy families to unhappy families. You may want to contrast biological families to families united by affection. Or if you think all of the families exemplify a similar feeling or value, you can discuss them one at a time, focusing on that common feature. Your opening sentence should state whatever pattern you are examining. Then work through the examples you have listed, referring to specific scenes in the book. In your final paragraph, tie this pattern into the themes and values of the book as a whole.

15. Begin by writing about actual objects and scenes that are bright or dark, such as Silas' bright gold, Molly's dark vial of opium, Silas' paleness, Eppie's and Godfrey's blond hair, Silas' bright cottage, or the Casses' dark parlor. Discuss what value each of these objects has in the plot—good, bad, dangerous, precious, etc. Then move to a more abstract level and discuss how various scenes are pictured as bright or dark. For example, the robbery of Silas' gold is a dark night scene, but his afternoons in the meadow with Eppie are light. Finally, examine the use of bright and dark as concepts in the book. For example, Godfrey speaks of Nancy as his bright hope, Silas talks about the dark mystery of his fate, and Dolly talks about the light shed by religion. If you see a definite pattern to all this imagery, define it in your final paragraph. If you don't, discuss the effect

upon the novel of a pattern of imagery that's constantly changing.

Test 2
1. B 2. C 3. B 4. B 5. A 6. C
7. A 8. C 9. B 10. A

11. First, outline Silas' cycle of fortune by briefly summarizing his story. Discuss which incidents mark his lowest points and which are his highest points. Analyze briefly the novel's symmetry. Then discuss the ways in which Silas seems a victim of circumstance. These may include his mysterious trances, the random treachery of others (such as William Dane and Dunstan), and the accidents that lead to his fatal events (such as his leaving his door open). In your next paragraph, discuss the ways in which Silas controls his fate. Talk here about conscious decisions he makes (to go away with his door unlocked, to keep the baby Eppie) and about features of his personality, such as his trusting nature, his miserliness, or his withdrawal from human companionship. Depending upon which examples persuade you most, finish with a paragraph arguing your case one way or the other. Show how the themes of the book support your case—do they show human beings as victims or as responsible creatures?

12. Begin by summarizing the events of Godfrey's story. Point out how it intersects with Silas' story. Then devote a paragraph to describing in detail Godfrey's personality in Part One. Discuss what Eliot says about him and how other characters regard him. Analyze his mental and emotional state during dramatized scenes. Refer to specific actions which reveal his character (such as letting Dunstan sell Wildfire or rushing into the snow in dancing shoes). In the next paragraph, describe Godfrey in Part Two. Again, look at all the various ways the author presents him to you. Emphasize how he's changed since Part One and how he hasn't changed. For example, he now speaks of God instead of fortune, but he still covers his selfish motives with a noble air when he offers to adopt Eppie. In your final paragraph, sum up how he's changed and discuss why these changes occurred.

13. Before writing, jot down the names of all the gentry characters you can remember. Try to group them in some pattern. For instance, you may want to write about the professionals, such as Kimble and Crackenthorpe, the good farmers, such as the Lammeters and Osgoods, and then the rural "first family," the Casses. Or you may want to talk about the younger generation—Godfrey, Dunstan, Nancy, Priscilla—as opposed to the older generation. You may want to discuss the men first and then the women. Deal with the strong families, the Lammeters and Osgoods, as opposed to weak families, the Casses and Kimbles. Write about the characters whom you think Eliot approves of first, and then discuss the characters you think she doesn't approve of. When you have chosen your pattern, begin your answer with a general statement about Eliot's view of this class. Then devote a paragraph to each separate cluster of characters you're discussing. In your final paragraph, define Eliot's moral values in this novel. Then show which gentry characters seem most in tune with those values.

14. In your opening sentence, define "the past"—familiar objects, personal memories, and traditions. Then devote a paragraph to examples of each category. Under familiar objects, you might discuss Silas' brown pot, the furze bush and stone-pit that Eppie cherishes, or the Squire's tankards at the Red House. Refer to specific

scenes which show what value these hold for certain characters. Under personal memories, discuss characters who cling to their memories, such as Silas, Eppie, Mr. Macey, or Nancy. Discuss how these characters are psychologically affected by their memories. Show how, in some cases, this changes the plot. Under traditions, talk about the traditions of Raveloe and how the community preserves them. In your final paragraph, define the value of the past in this novel. What other themes does it tie in with? How is it related to the novel's setting and tone?

15. Make two lists, side by side, of details describing the city and the village. Find parallels and contrasts in those two lists. If it helps, focus your thinking on two parts of the book: when Silas first comes to Raveloe and compares it to his hometown, and thirty-two years later when Silas returns to the city and sees it through new eyes. Look for differences on many levels: physical details, economic conditions, values, and social structures. In some cases, compare Raveloe directly with Lantern-Yard—for example, in contrasting their religious beliefs. In other cases, look at the city as a whole. For example, the Lantern-Yard sect is a small community trying to maintain its identity within the large urban area, while Raveloe is a tightly integrated community where everyone knows everybody else. Begin your answer with a general statement about the two settings of the book and how they fit into the plot. Then work through your list of examples. Whenever possible, show how Eliot seems to feel about these settings. In your final paragraph, define the historical significance of these two settings for the novel. Then express your own opinion about Eliot's purpose in contrasting them.

Term Paper Ideas and other Topics for Writing

Themes

1. Who do you think is "lucky" in this book? Who is "unlucky"? What role does luck play in the novel?

2. Compare Dolly's religion to Nancy's. Then compare the Raveloe religion to Silas' Lantern-Yard beliefs.

3. Discuss the aliens in this book: Silas Marner, the first Mr. Lammeter, Cliff the London tailor, the Misses Gunn, the gypsy peddler.

4. How does Eliot contrast the social classes in this novel? How does she connect them?

Characters

1. Who do you think is the villain of this novel? Support your opinion.

2. Who do you think is the hero of this novel? Support your opinion.

3. Compare William Dane and Dunstan Cass.

4. Compare Dolly Winthrop and Priscilla Lammeter.

5. Compare Godfrey and his brother Dunstan.

6. Compare Nancy and Eppie.

Scenes

1. Discuss the episode where Silas breaks his brown pot. Why is this an important scene?

2. Discuss how and why Eliot introduces you to Nancy by showing her with the Misses Gunn.

3. Analyze Chapter 6, the conversation at the Rainbow. What does this show you about the individuals there? What does it show you about Raveloe in general?

Technique

1. Discuss the symmetry of this novel.

2. Trace the plant imagery throughout the book. How does it relate to the themes?

3. Analyze the author's commentary voice. Do you think this adds to or detracts from the story? Defend your opinion.

4. How does Eliot use dialect in this novel? What effect does it create?

Research Topics

1. Read the book of Job in the Bible. Compare this story to *Silas Marner*.

2. Read Wordsworth's poem "Michael" and show how it influenced George Eliot in *Silas Marner*.

3. Read Shakespeare's play *The Winter's Tale* and discuss parallels between it and *Silas Marner*.

Creative Writing

1. Write a newspaper article for the *Raveloe Voice*, reporting on Silas Marner's robbery.

2. Write the story of Silas finding Eppie as Mr. Macey might tell it.

3. Write a version of Godfrey's will, telling his secret about Eppie.

Further Reading

CRITICAL WORKS

Biographies

Cross, J. W. *The Life of George Eliot*. New York: Amis Press, Inc., 1965. (First published London 1884.) The "official" biography, by Eliot's husband, edits her journals, letters, and conversations to give an admiring view of her life.

Haight, Gordon S. *George Eliot: A Biography*. New York: Oxford University Press, 1968. The standard biography, by perhaps the most influential Eliot scholar.

Hanson, Lawrence & Elisabeth. *Marian Evans and George Eliot*. London: Oxford University Press, 1952. Readable, reliable, and insightful.

Laski, Marghanita. *George Eliot and Her World*. New York: Charles Scribner's Sons, 1973. Well illustrated.

Redinger, Ruby V. *George Eliot: The Emergent Self*. New York: Alfred A. Knopf, 1975. An in-depth psychological study of Eliot's formative years, up to the writing of *Silas Marner*.

General Criticism

Leavis, F. R. *The Great Tradition*. New York: New York University Press, 1964. A study of the major authors of English literature, paying great attention to Eliot.

Praz, Mario. *The Hero in Eclipse in Victorian Fiction*. London: Oxford University Press, 1956. How the concept of the "hero" changed through Eliot's work and others'.

Showalter, Elaine. *A Literature of Their Own*. Princeton, N.J.: Princeton University Press, 1977. A study of women writers of the nineteenth and twentieth centuries.

Wagenknecht, Edward. *Cavalcade of the English Novel*. New

York: Henry Holt and Company, 1954. Places Eliot in context of Victorian literature.

Anthologies of Eliot Criticism

Carroll, David, ed. *George Eliot: The Critical Heritage*. New York: Barnes & Noble, Inc., 1971. Reviews written when Eliot's works first appeared.

Creeger, George R., ed. *George Eliot: A Collection of Critical Essays*. Englewood Cliffs, N.J.: Prentice-Hall, Inc., 1970. A selection of modern views.

Haight, Gordon S. *A Century of George Eliot Criticism*. Boston: Houghton Mifflin Company, 1965. Major critical articles on Eliot, from 1865 to 1965.

Hardy, Barbara, ed. *Critical Essays on George Eliot*. London: Routledge & Kegan Paul, 1970. Several good essays—note Lilian Haddakin's on *Silas Marner*.

Stang, Richard, ed. *Discussions of George Eliot*. Boston: D.C. Heath and Company, 1960. Includes most of the important essays on Eliot and her works.

Books on Eliot

Ashton, Rosemary. *George Eliot*. Oxford: Oxford University Press, 1983. Particularly good on Eliot's intellectual influences.

Bennett, Joan. *George Eliot: Her Mind and Art*. Cambridge: Cambridge University Press, 1948. A sensitive and sensible book, full of insights.

Hardy, Barbara. *The Novels of George Eliot*. New York: Oxford University Press, 1959. A major study of Eliot's form and structure.

Harvey, W. J. *The Art of George Eliot*. New York: Oxford University Press, 1969. Valuable look at Eliot's techniques.

Knoepflmacher, W. C. *George Eliot's Early Novels*. Berkeley and Los Angeles: University of California Press,

1968. A study of Eliot's literary development, up through *Silas Marner*.

Thale, Jerome. *The Novels of George Eliot*. New York: Columbia University Press, 1959. A thoughtful study, especially good on *Silas Marner*.

AUTHOR'S OTHER WORKS

Scenes of Clerical Life (1858) Three stories of provincial English characters.

Adam Bede (1859) The tragic love of a young carpenter for a vain, thoughtless country girl.

The Mill on The Floss (1860) A semi-autobiographical novel about a country childhood and young womanhood.

Romola (1862–63) A novel about a failed love affair between a morally serious young woman and a gifted but corrupt young man, set in fifteenth-century Florence.

Felix Holt (1866) Politics of the Industrial Revolution set off a plot about inheritance and family secrets.

The Spanish Gypsy (1868) A verse drama.

Middlemarch (1871–72) A rich social novel, possibly her masterpiece, analyzing love and life in an English provincial town.

Daniel Deronda (1875) A realistic view of upperclass marriage interwoven with a young man's conversion to Jewish political activism.

The Impressions of Theophrastus Such (1878) A volume of essays.

Glossary

Athanasian Creed A Christian creed defining belief in the holy Trinity and the incarnation of God in Christ.

110   A Step Beyond

bakehus Dialect: "bakehouse." A building or room where an oven is made available for baking.

catalepsy A state of temporary paralysis and loss of sensation.

chines A cut of meat from around the backbone.

collogue Dialect: "conspire."

colly Dialect: "to make black as coal."

'cute Dialect: "acute." Perceptive, sharp, clever.

doubt Dialect: "suspect."

farrier One who attends to or shoes horses. A blacksmith.

furze A spiny evergreen shrub with yellow flowers.

fustian A sturdy cloth made of coarse linen and cotton, dyed a dull color, usually worn by the working class.

hack A light saddle horse.

joseph A long riding cloak worn by ladies in the eighteenth century (old-fashioned by the time of *Silas Marner*).

lard-cakes Small flat cakes made of dough, lard, sugar, and spice, not a delicacy but a treat for country folk.

Mant's Bible A three-volume edition of the Bible, published in 1816, with explanatory notes and maps.

mawkin Dialect: "scarecrow."

moithered Dialect: "broken into small flakes." Bewildered, worried.

mole-catcher Someone who exterminated pesky field moles for farmers and then sold the valuable mole skins for a profit. Often, mole-catchers also did some illegal poaching on the side.

Old Harry The Devil.

orts Scraps of food, leftovers.

parish-clerk A layman who assists the minister during church services.

piert Dialect: "peart." Brisk, lively, cheerful, healthy.

pillion A pad attached behind a saddle for a second rider.

scrat Dialect: "scratch." To struggle for a living.

'sizes Dialect: "assizes." The sessions of superior court in English counties.

springe Dialect: "active, supple."

sodger Dialect: "soldier."

throstle A song thrush.

tinder-box A little metal box holding tinder and a flint and steel for lighting a fire.

The Critics

On the Characters

The art and originality in the story lies in the completely innocent cast given to the miserliness of the old weaver, his almost entire freedom from any touch of moral responsibility for the growth of this passion, and in the complete and unresisted revulsion of feeling caused by the loss of his gold and the substitution of a living interest in its place. Silas Marner's character is no common conception.

—R. H. Hutton, review in The Economist, 1861

In all those of our author's books which have borne the name of the hero or heroine—*Adam Bede, Silas Marner, Romola,* and *Felix Holt*—the person so put forward has really played a subordinate part. The author may have set out with the intention of maintaining him supreme; but her material has become rebellious in her hands, and the technical hero has been eclipsed by the real one.... Godfrey Cass, with his life-long secret, is by right the hero of *Silas Marner*."

—Henry James, Atlantic Monthly, 1866

George Eliot's concentration on the moral side of human nature is the chief source of her peculiar glory, the kernel of her precious unique contribution to our literature. Her imagination is not a dis-

torting glass like Dickens', vitalizing her figures by accentuating their personal idiosyncracies, nor is it, like Charlotte Brontë's, a painted window suffusing them with the color of her own live temperament; it is an X-ray, bringing them to life by the clearness with which she penetrates to the secret mainspring of their actions.
—*David Cecil*, Victorian Novelists, *1935*

(George Eliot) was more aware than her immediate predecessors of the complexity of characters and her creations cannot be labelled good or bad, nor accorded the wholesale approval or disapproval of the reader as readily as can many Victorian heroes or heroines.
—*Joan Bennett*, George Eliot: Her Mind and Art, *1948*

George Eliot can make the apparently simple mind as interesting as the sophisticated and more inventively creative mind of the artist. Nothing in the human imagination was alien to her imagination.
—*Barbara Hardy*, Particularities: Readings in George Eliot, *1982*

On the Setting

Nothing can be more profound than this picture of the manner in which all human beings are influenced by their environment . . . on laying down the book we do not dwell upon Silas Marner or Godfrey Cass or Dolly Winthrop, or any particular character, but are forced to embrace them all with all their restricted country life. Nothing short of Raveloe satisfies the memory.
—*Unsigned review in* Westminster Review, *1861*

We feel that there must be a silent guest in the chimney-corner of the 'Rainbow,' so thoroughly at home with the natives as to put no stress upon their behaviour, and yet one who has travelled out of sight of the village spire, and known the thoughts and feelings which are stirring in the great world outside.

—*Leslie Stephen*, Cornhill *magazine*, *1881*

On the Realism
We seem to be looking at . . . any of those domestic or rustic paintings of the Dutch school, where every leaf in the elm trees or the limes is painted, every gnarl of the bark inscribed, every rut followed with fidelity. We follow the people out of the hedgerows and the lanes into the kitchen. We see the endless meals, the eternal cup of tea; and the dog rests his head on our boot or flies barking to the yard, while young children toddle in and out of the drama at the least convenient moments.

—*V. S. Pritchett*, The Living Novel, *1947*

On George Eliot's Essential Qualities
Another striking thing (about George Eliot's writing) is the sense of gravity attached to an evil intention or to a failure of resolution, which because of the interdependence of mankind spreads its fatal repercussions in every direction; and another, the sense of the mysterious greatness of human life and the life of nature, the solemn mysteries in which we play a part while knowing no more about them than does the growing flower.

—*Marcel Proust*, Contre Sainte-Beuve, *collected 1954*

On Her Ideas
George Eliot's revolt against her inherited faith was based on intellectual grounds alone. At no time was there a moral revolt. It was inevitable, therefore, that, being what she was, she should have spent

the rest of her life trying to preserve the Christian morality without supernatural sanctions.
>—Edward Wagenknecht, Cavalcade of the English Novel, 1954

For most of us *Silas Marner* evokes painful memories of literature forced down our throats in the second year of high school. We were probably right in disliking it then, for it is an adult's book. . . . it is a serious and intelligent treatment of human life and conduct.
>—Jerome Thale, The Novels of George Eliot, 1959

NOTES

NOTES

NOTES

NOTES